Information and Communications Technology in Primary Schools

Children
or Computers
in Control?

Second Edition

RICHARD AGER

London: David Fulton, 2003

1843120429

 David Fulton Publishers

David Fulton Publishers Ltd
The Chiswick Centre, 414 Chiswick High Road, London W4 5TF

www.fultonpublishers.co.uk

First published in Great Britain in 2000 by David Fulton Publishers
Second edition published 2003

10 9 8 7 6 5 4 3 2

David Fulton Publishers is a division of Granada Learning Limited, part of Granada plc.

British Library Cataloguing in Publication Data
A catalogue record for this book is available from the British Library.

ISBN 1-84312-042-9

Typeset by FiSH Books, London
Printed and bound in Great Britain

Contents

Acknowledgements

I would like to thank my colleagues past and present from the ICT Curriculum team at Education Walsall, from the Leicestershire Consortium – NOF ICT Training Provider and from the Faculty of Education of the University of Central England in Birmingham who, both knowingly and unknowingly, have contributed to this book as a result of many discussions and informal conversations over the past few years. I am grateful to the many teachers I have observed working in schools, or who have attended in-service courses I have run, as it is they who have helped to inform my views on many of the ICT issues discussed in this book. I am also indebted to the many students I have worked with in schools on ICT curriculum development work. Much of the practical advice in this book is based on their research findings related to innovative teaching and learning strategies utilising ICT.

I would like to thank Gareth, Jenny, Sarah and Siân for the advice and support they have given to me on a number of ICT projects. Although they used to seek my advice on using computers they are now autonomous users of the technology, with e-mails being sent from the other side of the world and extremely fast fingerwork being used to send text messages.

I also reflect that lifelong learning is a reality when I consider that my dad, at eighty, after being introduced to ICT only a few years ago, is now an everyday user of the Internet for on-line shopping, on-line banking and communicating with his friends all over the country.

Finally, I would like to express my gratitude to Ann for her support and encouragement throughout both the writing and the revision of this book..

Richard Ager

Introduction

This book aims to provide teachers and student teachers with a basic introduction to the use of ICT in primary schools. In each chapter I have posed a series of questions that are regularly asked by teachers and trainee teachers. I hope that this will make it easy for you to access particular pieces of information. In many chapters I have also identified the main teaching and learning issues that need to be considered, in an attempt to emphasise the most important reasons why we should be using ICT in the primary classroom.

Throughout this book I have deliberately excluded reference to specific software titles or to particular operating systems and computers, although I have assumed that everyone will be using a computer with a graphical user interface (such as Windows 3.1, Windows 98, Macintosh or Acorn). I have preferred to discuss the generic characteristics of software because, although during the life of this book many new sophisticated software titles will be introduced, they will still be able to be described in terms of one of the nine basic forms of software as described in Chapter 5. It is, after all, the features that are important, not the titles.

For example Microsoft Excel is sold as a spreadsheet application, but it can be used very successfully as a database. Microsoft Word is a word processor, but has many features associated with a desktop publishing program. Junior Pinpoint is a piece of software that analyses data input in the form of a questionnaire. This is a hybrid desktop publishing (questionnaire design) and database (graphical representation of findings) package and removes the necessity to produce a database structure consisting of fields and records. In general, new pieces of software allow you to do things that you can do with your existing software, but in a much easier way.

The important thing to remember as far as ICT in primary schools is concerned is to talk about the packages with reference to their generic facilities, rather than their commercial names. Then you will be sure that children are learning and developing all the ICT techniques and skills that are currently necessary.

The premise on which the book is written is that the child can be in control of the computer, or the computer can be in control of the child. I do not believe that we should, or even need to, concentrate on one or other of the approaches to the exclusion of the other, but it is important that we understand the implications for children of the approach we use. The computer is an incredibly powerful machine, and I hope this book will help you to use it as effectively as possible to enhance children's teaching and learning experiences.

Why All This Concern about ICT?

In his book *Visions*, Michio Kaku (1998) quotes Mark Weiser from Xerox Palo Alto Research Center in Silicon Valley as saying, 'Long-term, the PC and workstation will wither because computing access will be everywhere: in the walls, on wrists, and in "scrap computers" (like scrap paper) lying about to be grabbed as needed.' As it was at this research centre that the modern PC was virtually invented, together with the laser printer and the program that was the foundation for all subsequent graphical user interfaces (such as Windows), a vision such as Weiser's should not be lightly dismissed.

We have seen rapid developments in the status of information and communications technology (ICT) in primary schools over the past ten years and we are also witnessing the birth of some new terminology, that of e-learning. Charles Clarke, Secretary of State for Education, stated in July 2003:

> A great deal of progress has been made so far, but there is much more to do. E-learning can take us a further step forward. This is about embedding and exploiting technologies in everything we do, and getting ICT embedded across the curriculum for all subjects and in all pedagogues. E-learning has the power to transform the way we learn, and to bring high quality accessible learning to everyone – so that every learner can achieve his or her potential.
>
> (DfES 2003a)

A definition of this new term is also provided in the same document. 'If someone is learning in a way that uses information and communication technologies, they are using e-learning.' So after six years there is no lessening of government will to embed ICT into all aspects of education.

Excellence in Schools, the first White Paper of the new Labour government (or should this be the New Labour government?) stated, 'We are determined to create a society where, within ten years, information and communications technology (ICT) has permeated every aspect of education' (DfEE 1997).

In a speech to the annual National Union of Teachers conference a year later, the then Secretary of State for Education, David Blunkett, said, 'Optional ready-made schemes of work are being produced that will ensure that each year teachers do not have to "reinvent the wheel" as they prepare their classwork.' And we are now all very familiar with the Qualifications and Curriculum Authority (QCA) Schemes of Work and all the other optional materials that have been produced for both the numeracy and literacy strategies and that will undoubtedly be produced by the newly coordinated Primary Strategy.

And the Labour government has ensured that ICT in education has remained high on the DfES's agenda. There is a renewed emphasis on using ICT to enhance the quality of children's teaching and learning experiences in schools, building upon children's ability to use the ICT tools effectively. So why are developments in schools still happening rather slowly?

What is preventing the rapid effective development of ICT in primary schools?

During the 1980s and 1990s computers arrived in schools because they were seen to be 'a good thing'. In the same way that the invention of a material which could be used to produce small, lightweight, high-quality headphones led to the development of the Sony Walkman, the development of computers led us to think about the ways in which their power could be used in the educational environment. It was not a case of teachers saying 'What we really need to enhance children's teaching and learning is a piece of equipment that will do this', it was politicians wanting to be seen to be enhancing educational facilities who provided funding for computers that went into schools. We have done our bit – now see how they can be used to enhance your teaching. Although funding was provided for much development work, and a great deal was done, the fact that it was done the wrong way round is perhaps the reason why it took so long to integrate ICT work into all schools. Neither were developments helped when much of the LEA support structure was removed in the early 1990s due to further government directives. So by the end of the 1990s training was needed, but unfortunately, for many teachers, what they got was not the training they wanted.

The New Opportunities Fund (NOF) ICT Training programme was developed to equip all teachers with the knowledge, skills and understanding to make sound decisions about when, when not and how to use ICT effectively in teaching particular subjects. It was attempting to respond to a need that teachers had for relevant training in the use of ICT. There were concerns that the training money would get into the hands of the traditional ICT training companies, so that everyone would know how to do a mail merge and how to manipulate some graphics, but they would not be able to use ICT to enhance children's teaching and learning experience in the classroom. For this reason, in their contract, the training providers had to concentrate on how ICT could be used to enhance teaching and learning and were prohibited from teaching basic ICT software skills as part of a NOF-funded package. To avoid large sums of money being used to cover staff absence on these courses it was also decided that no NOF funds could be used to release teachers for the training. So although some schools successfully built the ICT training into their continuing professional development (CPD) programmes using training days to cover some of the training, the message in other schools was that all the training had to be done in teachers' own time.

For teachers who needed basic ICT skills, discussions about how to use software to enhance children's learning were a little abstract. And in schools where the ICT software and hardware was very limited, these same teachers found that they did not have time to work with their children on computers anyway. It is unsurprising that a major initiative costing £230 million pounds failed to achieve all that it might have done when it took little account of the lessons of successful CPD over the past twenty years. Most significant among these would be that the training should be immediately relevant to teachers, that they should have some ownership over it and that it should be perceived as important by senior management as an integral part of the school's development plan. NOF training was generally successful only in schools where senior managers acted in a positive way to make it work.

In 2003 we have substantial funding for the hardware, software and network infrastructure, a fully trained workforce with opportunities through a number of initiatives to develop their ICT skills further, the support of an advisory teacher or consultant team in all LEAs as part of the Primary Strategy (where ICT is now a major focus together with literacy and numeracy), leadership training that focuses upon the importance of ICT to improve both administration and teaching and learning, and a government that is fully committed to the transformational role that, it is believed, ICT can have in primary schools. As Charles Clarke says, 'My vision is one where schools are confidently, successfully and routinely exploiting ICT alongside other transformational measures. By doing so they will be delivering an education that equips learners for life in the Information Age of the 21st century' (DfES 2003b). So what are we waiting for?

What features of ICT support teaching and learning in subjects?

The Teacher Training Agency documentation (TTA 1998) relating to the needs analysis for NOF training identifies four functions of ICT that can be used by teachers to achieve subject teaching and learning objectives. Although NOF training has now finished, the features are still relevant and important. These are the speed and automatic functions of ICT, the capacity and range of ICT, the provisional nature of information when stored and presented using ICT and the interactive way in which information can be used when using ICT. Let us look at these features a little more closely.

Speed and automatic functions of ICT

In a primary classroom it would be difficult to record the outside temperature over a period of 24 hours. This would be logistically problematic, and discussions about the graph and the size of the axes would then confuse many younger children. But the concept of temperature, and the idea that it changes as the day goes by, is one that is relevant to everyday life, and has lots of uses.

By using a remote sensor attached to a computer, it is possible to collect the data, and to allow children to manipulate it using different chart styles and then to be given opportunities to analyse it. In this way we are developing some analytical skills, with children relating their real-life experiences about temperature to a graphical representation, when previously the actual physical construction of the graph would have been time-consuming, and very much of a 'following instructions' type activity, and one that would have got in the way of the actual understanding.

The fact that routine tasks can now be completed and repeated quickly allows children to concentrate on higher-order thinking and tasks. This means that interpretation skills must be taught and developed at much earlier ages than previously.

Capacity and range

Suppose you were to hold a competition between two pairs of children in the classroom. One pair has access to the school library's encyclopaedia, while the others are sitting in front of a computer loaded with a CD-ROM based encyclopaedia. If you ask them to find out a piece of factual information, and provided that both pairs are competent in the appropriate skills of using either a paper based or a CD-ROM based encyclopaedia, then you will not be surprised that the ICT group find the answer first.

Speech coming out of a computer is now commonplace, and words can be spoken and highlighted in a way that previously could have been done only with one-to-one teaching between an adult and a child.

Powerful computers are now able to produce very lifelike simulations, the most well known of which simulate flying and landing aircraft at a range of international airports. Here children are able to undertake a range of manoeuvres in a context that they would be extremely unlikely ever to be in, but they do it in complete safety. While this particular example has limited direct educational benefit, other simulations do exist.

Difficult ideas are made more understandable when ICT makes them visible. Consider how you might explain electric current flow in a simple circuit. You might draw a diagram on the whiteboard, or show a diagram in a book, but an animation on the computer screen or interactive whiteboard, which can be quickly transformed to a second and third circuit, can clearly help children, and adults, to understand quite difficult concepts.

One of the enormous advantages that ICT now has is the way in which it can incorporate so many different media in one machine. A typical multimedia application will include voices, text, drawing and photographic images, music, sound effects and video. This immediately provides teachers with an extremely powerful teaching tool.

The use of the Internet in primary schools brings with it a whole series of challenges. There is more information on the Internet than anyone can possibly cope with. Anyone can set up a website, and there is no requirement that the information on it is true or even legal. In reading a book, you are at least fairly sure that the material will have been read by a number of editors, and that the publishers would be responsible for gross factual errors and would therefore remove them. When children start to use websites, they need to be aware that just because it says so on the screen, it is not necessarily true. The idea that facts need to be checked, and to come from two or three different sources, is an idea that some primary school children will need to be introduced to. They need to be able to think about the credibility of the information, and what quality control there is over it.

It will be increasingly possible to link up with 'experts' using e-mail communication or video-conferencing, so that children can experience some personalised feedback to queries they have. Again, care must be taken to weigh up the practicalities against the hyperbole of such approaches. While it is easy to envisage how children may access a website on a particular topic that has been specially designed for children, and to gain answers to their questions from there, the enormity of a structure that would have an 'expert' at the end of an e-mail line to answer, on an individual basis, queries that children may have is difficult to envisage. The possibility that another 'expert' would be permanently available 'on tap' via a video-conference link is even more unlikely.

Provisionality

The provisional nature of much of work using ICT has to be one of its strengths. There is no pressure to get things right the first time. You are able to put your thoughts down as they arrive and then to 'cut and paste' them into an appropriate order after reflection. If you are satisfied with a particular section of written work you do not have to copy it again and again as you move towards your finished product. I was reminded of how much I had become accustomed to using ICT in this way at a job interview at which I was asked to provide briefing papers for what would have been my line manager. On seeing the pen and paper before me I was not too concerned, but by the end of the hour I realised how the initial brainstorm of ideas on one sheet of paper, the draft structure on a second and the final response on a third contained so many sections that were similar, but in the wrong order. I did not get the job!

I am sure children feel more inclined to draft, redraft and redraft again if each time it does not mean starting with another fresh sheet of paper. And certainly this book would never have been written if I did not have access to a powerful word processor that allowed me to change, change and change again! And you will never see where I made the typing errors or where I made glaring mistakes when I first put 'finger to key'.

But the teacher must also be sensitive to the child's individual strengths, feelings and motivation. There may be times when children do not produce a perfect piece of work, but it is clear they have achieved a much higher standard than they had done previously. You must use your professional judgement to decide that a further request to redraft might well demotivate and diminish the obvious success and pride that the child has.

Interactivity

There is evidence that the interactive nature of computer technology motivates and stimulates learning. In particular, the immediate feedback that can be provided in response to questions when given by a computer is perceived by the child to lack the value judgements that may be present when a teacher marks some work. The work can be seen to be right or wrong, not good or bad!

Using a CD-ROM encyclopaedia to find some information can be a very interactive experience. Starting with one word, the children are provided with too many articles, and this then leads them to look for other strategies. They can choose to select a particular area of knowledge (literature or science), a particular period of time (seventeenth or twentieth century) or a particular medium (sound or video clips), and on each selection they see the range of articles changing. Similarly with a spreadsheet, a change in a single value, over which the child can have control, can cause huge knock-on changes throughout the spreadsheet.

How should I decide whether to use an ICT approach or an alternative?

Effective evaluation skills are vital for teachers. On a daily basis teachers make split second decisions, which need to be based on evidence. This they evaluate and then come to a conclusion as to the next form of action. A vital part of the education of trainee teachers is assisting them to develop these evaluative skills – clearly an educative activity rather than a training one.

Let us explore a few aspects of evaluation in the field of ICT. A teacher has a wide range of technology that could be used, e.g. television and radio, tape recorders, video, computers, e-mail, the Internet, digital cameras, digital video cameras and scanners. In order to make an appropriate selection the teacher needs to think very carefully about the possibilities. Some obviously have practical implications: 'The tape recorder has broken', 'We haven't got a scanner' and 'The television is booked at the time I want to use it' are typical examples. But then consider the content. You have a video and a CD-ROM on the same basic topic. The video can be shown to the whole class at once. If you use the CD-ROM the children will need to work in pairs on the two computers in the classroom. The implication, even at this initial stage, is that using the video would be much quicker – a class lesson followed by some group work – than the use of a computer – pairs working over a period of three or four weeks. But what about the implications for learning? The video requires little interaction. All the children see the same thing. What are you expecting them to get out of the video? Are they able to make notes as they watch? Are they given a focus before watching?

If it is a 'good' CD-ROM then it will engage the children, and they will be able to interact with the ideas and information available. They may be able to choose different approaches and to find out information about which they are particularly interested. They may, however, need time to be taught how to use the equipment, and will need to be supported throughout the activity. You will need to know when to intervene to ensure that the activity is a worthwhile learning experience for the children.

You will also need to have evaluated the content of the video and the content and navigation of the CD-ROM. Are they appropriate for the learning objectives that you have in mind? Clearly if they use a CD-ROM they will need to be aware of ICT skills such as search strategies. Do they already know how to do this, or will each pair need to be taught prior to them engaging in the activity? Perhaps it is the factual knowledge that is important in this activity. Should you give clear instructions to each pair of children as to which words to look up on the CD-ROM so that they quickly get to the 'relevant' information? If you do this, have you taken away all the ICT element of the activity? Isn't it just the same as handing them a book open at the appropriate page and telling them to read it?

This is the sort of evaluative activity in which you need to engage to decide on a particular approach for one activity! Fortunately, one skill that is part of being a professional is that these thoughts happen so quickly and decisions are made so swiftly that you almost react instinctively. This is what initial teacher education (ITE) and CPD are about, and teachers become more competent throughout their career as they develop these instinctive reactions. But this is based on a firm foundation and a clear understanding of the issues involved. Many existing teachers, despite NOF training, do not have the underlying knowledge, skills and confidence in both the technology and pedagogy of ICT that they might have in their own subject specialism, and therefore this evaluative process is initially more difficult. So how do you actually become more competent?

The stages of becoming competent in your use of ICT

If you are unaware both that computers exist and that they can be used to enhance teaching and learning in the primary curriculum then you are in a state of *unconscious incompetence*. The first stage of your development would be to see good practice in operation and to read details about specific activities that are seen to be effective in a wide variety of scenarios. You now see what ICT has to offer, but still feel ill prepared to deal with it. You are in a state of *conscious incompetence*. You are now encouraged to attend a short course that deals with some very practical issues, and gives you details of how to manage a small number of ICT activities and the learning gains that can be achieved. You try them out in the classroom and are pleased with their success. You are beginning to feel confident with this particular package. You have now reached *conscious competence*. You try out the ideas again, each time developing them a little. You see the opportunity for using the same approach in other work, and you integrate ICT within your planning as a matter of course. You now do not consider ICT as something particularly special. You are now *unconsciously competent*.

This process will continue as you develop other areas of ICT. Initially you are unaware of the nature of a virtual learning environment (*unconscious incompetence*). Your school becomes interested in the idea and sets up an after-school meeting with one of the suppliers (*conscious incompetence*). You are provided with a one-day training session on how to use the software and team meetings are set up in order to plan for the introduction of the virtual learning environment next school year (*conscious competence*). After evaluating the year's work you happily incorporate and extend the use of the virtual learning environment into the work of other year groups (*unconsciously competent*).

This process can be applied to any new idea that you need to be involved in, and is useful in helping to identify what you need to do in order to get to the next stage. It is the process of moving from unconscious or conscious incompetence through to unconscious competence that ITT courses and the training of existing teachers need to concentrate on, and the main thrust will need to be on the effective use of ICT to enhance children's teaching and learning.

Training or education

In the field of ICT there are clearly different activities, some of which relate to training and others to education. To put this into context, consider your eleven-year-old daughter coming home and telling you she had done 'sex education' at school today. You might be pleased that the school was discussing this issue in an appropriate context for your child. But now consider your reaction if your daughter came home and said that today she had 'sex training'!

Children (and students and teachers) need training in the use of ICT, in the same way that they need training in the use of a pencil, and later a pen as they develop their joined-up writing. ICT training in industry and commerce is characterised by exercises that enable you to practise opening up appropriate files and windows, pressing appropriate keys and printing out finished outcomes. You know how to set margins on a word processor, to set formulae in a spreadsheet, to edit a piece of clip art or to draw a square using a 'screen-based turtle' procedure. You then develop your skills in contexts that are more appropriate to your own interests or job requirements. You might design a database for your CD collection, or produce a template for the company's newsletter, and in doing so you start to ask questions. These are answered by the trainer, the software help system, a handbook or a colleague who has discovered how to achieve the desired effect.

Then you go back to work and develop your new ICT skills in tandem with your existing skills of management, personnel and selling. You know how to set up a spreadsheet, but now you are looking at the information itself. Which graphical format most easily demonstrates the trend in the data? Which is the most appropriate form in which to put the sales figures into the departmental newsletter in order to motivate the sales force? Before ICT you probably would not have had a weekly departmental newsletter. With it you are now having to develop some high-order thinking in order to analyse information that previously you did not have, and to consider the most effective way of presenting it to achieve your desired result. It is this sort of work that I think should concern us most in education.

What are the implications for schools of increasing home ownership of computers?

As home ownership of computers increases this is going to have a considerable influence on the sort of work that goes on in the classroom. Children have always been encouraged to read at home, and this has usually been possible as books could be taken home. A situation now exists where some children will have access to a computer and facilities that are of a higher standard than those available in school, and will have a higher level of technical skill. We must make use of these skills, and not treat everyone as operating at the same level.

Conversely, there may be children who clearly do not have access to computer facilities at home, so these skills will need to be developed solely in school, although increasingly funds are available to provide community access to computers in libraries, in city learning centres, in community centres and out-of-hours in schools to eliminate any possible digital divide.

Children are likely to be enthusiastic and confident about using computers and it would be a pity to lose any of this natural curiosity by going back to basics! The experience and skill that they have must be acknowledged and built upon. Peer tutoring is a successful strategy, and should not be dismissed as assisting a less skilled child by wasting the more able child's time. As we all know, teaching something to someone else makes us think very carefully about the knowledge and skills that we want to transmit, and on reflecting upon this, we ourselves come to have a clearer understanding.

In some cases it is likely that a child's home use of computers may be solely for playing games. The perseverance and problem-solving skills that children use while playing games should not be dismissed as having no educational value, and it is also likely that they are able to think and act quickly – they need to if they are to reach the next level of the game.

Children need to be encouraged to use the computer for more sophisticated activities. We will all have experienced a child, having being asked to do a project on a particular historical figure, returning to school with two or three pages of well presented text and a picture of the person, saying they did it on their computer at home. At first glance this is a very commendable effort, but you then realise that the whole thing is taken from a CD-ROM based encyclopaedia or the Internet, and involved a very simple search, cutting and pasting the text and picture into a blank document, and printing it out. This child has demonstrated ICT capability in the technicalities of using a computer, but in producing the product has learned nothing about the historical figure, and therefore has failed to achieve your learning objective. The task you set needs to be more clearly structured so that the child has to interact with the text in a meaningful way, and produce a more useful piece of work.

What technical things do I need to know?

Terminology or jargon?

You may well drive a car to work most mornings. Would you be able to answer a few simple questions? How do you stop the car? How do you switch on the main headlamps? Where do you put in the petrol? These are easy. Where are the spark plugs? How do you change an indicator lamp? How do you check the amount of oil in the engine? These are still quite straightforward. What are the advantages of electronic ignition over a mechanical distributor arm? How does the internal combustion engine work? Perhaps these are a little more difficult. But in order to use your car effectively, you only need to know the answers to some of the earlier questions. Certainly, there will be enthusiasts who know the answers to all the questions, and they may well enjoy taking the engine to pieces to fine tune it or repair it. But it is not essential to using the car. Similarly with computers, you do not need to understand every detail of a computer specification in order to use it, although it is obviously helpful when you are buying one.

It is clearly important that professionals are able to communicate effectively about such an important element of their work as ICT, and in order to achieve this people must be aware of appropriate terminology. However, ICT experts are renowned for using TLAs (three letter acronyms) as a means of maintaining control and power over people who readily admit they do not understand the detailed workings of a modern computer system! Clearly they are related to the stereotypical garage mechanic who always seems to suck his teeth and explain that although it appears you only need a replacement gasket, it's certainly a lot more serious – and expensive – than that!

So children need to be taught about menus and mice, and the enter key and cells, rows and columns and cutting, copying and pasting, floppy and hard disks, CD-ROMs and screens as they are integral to their work with the computer applications themselves. But they, or you or I, are unlikely to have to understand the sort of jargon found in the following extract from a computer magazine.

SFT-III servers appear to break the rules for Ethernet by having LAN cards in each system and an interconnection via the MSL cards between two servers without passing through the hub. In fact, if you plug in an SFT-III pair into a modem switch you will be able to see the two servers passing keep-alive packets to one another down their LAN connections at a rate of one per tick.

As the complexity of computer and network systems in schools increases, people with an appropriate technical background are being employed, either permanently or on a part-time or consultancy basis, to look after the technical aspects. ICT should be looked at in the same terms as electricity. You are happy to plug in an appliance to the mains, and switch on, but if a fault develops in the local sub-station, you wait for the electricity company, not climb over the fence with your screwdriver.

The basics

Computers now have a graphical user interface (GUI) (pronounced gooyey). This is also known as a WIMP environment, which means that the screen is made up of windows, icons, menus and pointers. Each program runs in its own window on the screen. Each program and many of each program's functions are represented by a small picture or icon. Programs have a list of words under the title bar of the program, and when you select one of these you get a whole series of options as on a menu. In order to select icons on the screen the computer has a pointer, which is controlled by a mouse, rollerball or other pointing device.

One of the powers of a WIMP environment is that programs look very similar, and often have common features. This means that when you can competently use one program, you do not need so much training in order to learn how to use another one. Let us take a very common feature, that of cutting, pasting and copying. Text or numbers in most computer applications can be selected (by clicking on the mouse button and moving the cursor over the section – it becomes highlighted). This is called 'click and drag'. Once the section is highlighted it can be copied, by pressing the copy button and then by moving the cursor to the position where you want the text to go and pressing the paste button. The text is now in two places in the document. If, instead of copying, you pressed the cut button, the selected material would have moved from the first place to the second position. This can also be done between applications. A common example of this would be copying the text of an e-mail and pasting it into a word processor to form the basis of a report. This process is used in most software packages, and can also be used to move files from one folder to another, or to get rid of them completely.

Standalone or networked

In the beginning, a PC computer sat by itself and was self-contained. All the software that would run on the machine was installed on its own hard disk or had to be loaded from floppy disk each time it was used. Ideally, each computer in the school should have the same software available so that they are completely flexible and can be used by anyone at any time. But in the real world this is unlikely. First, it is very time-consuming to set up every computer in exactly the same way; second, it is almost certain that some of your older computers will not be able to run some of the more recent software.

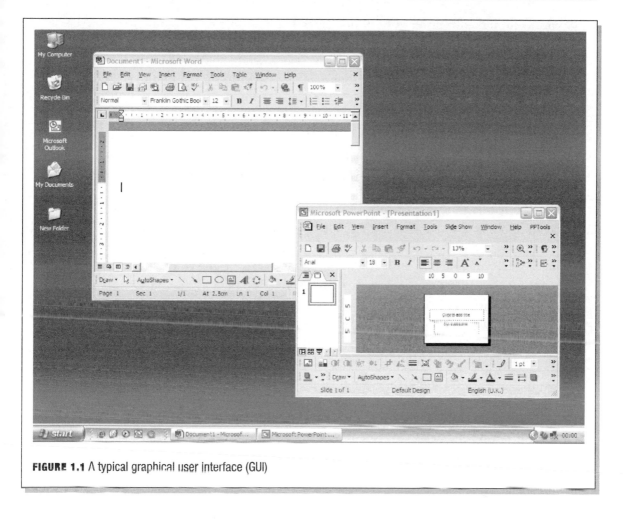

FIGURE 1.1 A typical graphical user interface (GUI)

One way round this problem is to have all the computers networked. This means connecting them all, using special cabling, to one bigger computer called a server. You put all the software once on to the server, and every time someone on a machine wishes to use it, instead of loading it from the hard disk in their own machine they load it from the server. This means that each computer will have available the same range of software, and when you buy a new piece of software it just needs to be installed once on the server – saving a great deal of time. The disadvantages of networking computers are the cost of the cabling, the restriction the cabling places on moving the computers around and the technical expertise required to set the computers up to work on a network. With newer wireless networks some of these problems can be alleviated.

New machines now typically have incredibly fast processors, gigantic hard disk drives, CD-ROM drives which are able not only to play CD-ROMs but also to write information on to writable CD-ROMS, and even larger storage devices such as DVD drives (digital versatile disk or digital video disk). They also can connect to peripherals (i.e. extra components that fit on to your computer, like printers, back-up drives, scanners and digital cameras) using USB2 connections. USB (universal serial bus) has the advantage that the data travels very quickly down the connecting wire, and in many cases it also powers the device itself, so you do not need the spaghetti-like tangle of three of four small power supplies around your computer. The computer is also able to identify what you are connecting, so it becomes a little like plugging a washing machine into a socket on the wall.

Because ICT is encouraged as a cross-curricular activity, you need to be very clear that the use of a particular ICT package is developing children's ICT capability, at the same time as covering an important element of another subject effectively and in an interesting way. If a child is word processing material for a history topic in Year 2, and word processing material for a different history topic in Year 6, in what ways is the word processing activity itself giving children an opportunity to demonstrate progression? Indeed, why are they word processing at all? Is it because they are making use of the drafting and redrafting facilities to produce some material for a particular audience, or are they just using the computer to 'type out' a neat copy of their work? Questions such as these are addressed in the chapters that look at possible activities for different subject areas.

As the speed with which information can travel along the improved cables from server to desktop machine increases, another option is available. This is the network computer rather than the personal computer. With this, more and more things are taken out of a PC until it becomes a keyboard, a monitor, speakers and a small piece of electronics, and all the other components are put into the server. In computer terminology, this is called a 'thin client, thick server'. The advantage is that the computer can be made much cheaper, and it would be of no use at all without being connected to a network – and therefore less liable to be stolen. An added advantage for a school environment is that it cannot be customised personally by the user. All these settings are made centrally at the server. We all know how much children like changing colour schemes!

There are also more opportunities for portable computer devices such as notebooks, personal digital assistants (PDAs) or even mobile phones to be used for learning. Many schools are currently using wireless networks and notebook computers so that children can carry their machines around and can be connected to the Internet and the school's own network without plugging in cables.

Once we have all the programs and data being delivered down the cable from the server, why do we need our own server? Why don't we load our software from the publisher's server using the new fast broadband network, charged on the basis of use or perhaps on a lease contract? You would easily be able to try out new programs by downloading them from suppliers' servers.

Similarly, why does your software need to be on your site. You will find that computer-based learning systems will become increasingly available for all subjects and using a range of teaching methods. Many of the new digital resources are on-line, meaning that they can be kept up-to-date (and the suppliers can charge you an annual subscription cost rather than a one-off payment). So children can download a mathematics teaching package, via the Internet, both at school and on their home computer, if they have one available, and work through the material at their own pace at any time they like. Those who have particular ability may be motivated to carry on with far more advanced work. Many schools are currently exploring these e-learning avenues.

What developments are just around the corner?

In 1998 Michio Kaku wrote that we were nearing the stage of ubiquitous computing. He believed that within ten years, a typical office, and probably classroom, would contain 100 *tabs*, 10 to 20 *pads* and one or two *boards*.

A tab is a tiny badge that everyone will wear and that includes an infra-red transmitter and has the power of a current PC. 'There are endless possibilities for computer tabs. They may be able to scan the Internet, and alert the wearer to crucial developments, to important calls and to family emergencies' (Kaku 1998). Imagine each of the children in your class wearing a tab and the use to which you could put that power. But if you consider it, many children now do have a device as powerful as some early PCs, which might also have an infra-red transmitter, but have you thought about using the power of your children's mobile phones to enhance teaching and learning in the classroom?

A pad resembles a very thin computer monitor. They will be used like blank sheets of paper, but each will be a fully operational PC.

> When we scribble on such smart paper, the graphics program inside will be able to convert our idle doodles into beautiful graphics or use editing capabilities to convert our notes into grammatically correct text. And after we are finished with it and have saved our work on the main computer, we simply toss it in the stack of pads on our desk.
>
> (Kaku 1998)

What keyboard and mouse skills will we need to teach children when working in this kind of environment? Not very many, by the sound of it. Yet already some schools are exploring the use of tablet PCs with children. A tablet PC consists of a screen that can be written on using a stylus, with all the traditional tools of a computer readily to hand. They have got a little way to go before they are as thin as paper and as recyclable, but much of the functionality is already there.

A board is a wall mounted computerised screen. It will act as a widescreen television, monitor, whiteboard and teleconference screen. Again it will be a powerful computer, with links to all the tabs and pads in the locality. This device is very nearly available. There are primary schools that have interactive whiteboards in every classroom, and as the price of plasma screens comes down it may not be too long before we can do away with the projection element all together.

Kaku's view was that, within a decade, the use of computers could be as all-pervading and as invisible as, for example, electricity currently is. I have little doubt that technically he is absolutely right, although with only five years to go I think that a little unlikely. It requires a wholesale belief by all teachers in all schools that the use of ICT is beneficial and that it will enhance teaching and learning and raise standards. Without that, however much money is provided for computers, software and training, a few committed and interested schools will forge their way to the very cutting edge of ICT use in schools, while the large majority of schools will remain in the backwater. Vast culture changes like this do not take place quickly.

Teachers need to see strategically how ICT can best be used. Schools need to decide whether computers should be used far more as a teaching machine – as a way of keeping track of children electronically, with the computer being in control of the child – or whether the children should use the machine for word-processing, spreadsheets and data analysis, and be in control of it.

The development of ICT in schools seems to me analogous with that of the rail system in the UK. When I visited the annual BETT show, a late train meant that I missed my connection and had to take a circuitous route that took much longer, and I had to pay an extra London underground train fare as well. On my return the train was crowded and many people had to stand for at least the first hour of the journey. However, in the corporate magazine there was a message from the owner of this particular train company acknowledging the problems but saying that with time and an enormous investment in both rolling stock and infrastructure all the problems would be solved. And to take the analogy further still, this incident happened five years ago, and on a similar journey a few weeks ago the train service was still abysmal, although I am told that somewhere there are a few really new trains running, which offer an excellent service.

With ICT in schools we have a very similar situation. Technically, we have the power and flexibility to do wonderful things for our children's education, and the amount of resourcing that has been provided from government specifically for ICT has been enormous. Schools have a continued source of funding for ICT hardware year on year, and a powerful and stable broadband infrastructure is being developed to connect all schools, giving them not only extremely fast access to the Internet but also the ability to download video clips and engage in video conferencing. Curriculum Online is providing schools with £100 million each year for the next three years specifically for digital content and £230 million was spent on a programme of CPD, giving every teacher in the country the opportunity to learn how to use ICT to enhance teaching and learning in their own phase and/or specialist area. Yet the latest indication is that only 15 per cent of schools seem to be making effective use of ICT to raise standards in a coherent, whole-school, strategic way. Like the trains, there are a few good ones, but they are few and far between.

The National College for School Leadership has developed a framework defining an e-confident school. The ten features are:

- high level of staff confidence, competence and leadership;
- re-engineered teaching, learning and assessment, integrating effective use;
- leading and managing distributed and concurrent learning;
- effective application within organisational and management processes;
- coherent personal learning development, support and access for all leaders, teaching and non-teaching staff;
- secure, informed professional judgement;

- appropriate resource allocation to ensure sustainable development;
- availability, access and technical support;
- pupils/students with high ICT capability;
- the school as the lead community learning and information hub (DfES 2003a).

In summary this means that to be e-confident a school needs a strong and clear leadership that sees ICT as a vital and integral part of a twenty-first-century learning establishment, to ensure that funding is spent effectively on ICT developments and a group of staff that all share the same vision.

Do you want to work in an e-confident school? If so, it is hoped that this book will help to shape your vision.

Teaching and Learning with ICT

In what way does ICT enhance teaching and learning?

There is no point using information and communications technologies if children do not receive an enhanced learning experience. Using the computer as a reward for finishing work off quickly or letting children play games on it at playtime hardly justify the expenses of a modern multimedia machine. The money spent on the machine could have greatly enhanced the school's library book provision.

There is increasing, but limited, evidence that suggests that standards improve in schools that use ICT. *Primary Schools – ICT and Standards* (BECTa 2003a) highlights these key research findings.

> High ICT schools outperformed low ICT schools in the same socio-economic group...Pupils' ICT attainment is generally independent of socio-economic circumstances.

This clearly implies that good socio-economic circumstances are not a prerequisite for effective use of ICT.

> Schools where ICT is used well within a subject tend to achieve better results in that subject than other schools...Generally there is a positive relationship between good ICT attainment and improved standards in English, mathematics and science, with those schools in less favourable circumstances showing a slightly more pronounced trend.

There is also evidence that the more subjects in which ICT is used within the curriculum the higher the standards that are achieved in both those subjects, and other subjects in which ICT is not used.

> Schools that combine good ICT resources with very good ICT teaching gain better results than those with good ICT resources but poor ICT teaching.

Here clearly the importance of good teachers who use ICT effectively is highlighted.

> Schools with good or very good leadership are nearly twice as likely to have good ICT resources than those with poor or unsatisfactory leadership, and those with good leadership are almost three times as likely to provide good ICT learning opportunities than those with satisfactory leadership.

Again this highlights how important the development of ICT is as a whole-school issue.

The document goes on to outline that there are five factors that need to be present to allow schools to develop good ICT learning opportunities in schools. These are:

- ICT resourcing;
- ICT leadership;
- ICT teaching;
- school leadership;
- general teaching.

If all five factors are present then there is a greater likelihood that good ICT learning opportunities will be present in the school.

If you want ICT in your school to have the maximum impact on teaching and learning it is clear that you need appropriate ICT resources, both hardware and software, effective leadership of ICT, highlighting the importance of the role of the ICT coordinator, exemplary teaching of both the ICT and all other subjects by all teachers and effective overall school leadership that takes into account e-learning developments.

How can ICT be managed in the primary classroom?

Let us take a simple scenario. You are, or are soon to be, a Year 4 class teacher. Your classroom will contain three PCs and you will also have a weekly timetabled session in the school's ICT suite of 16 machines. All machines have a basic range of word processing, database and spreadsheet software and you also have a large range of CD-ROM titles. All computers have Internet access through a broadband network, and you have a ceiling mounted digital projector that projects on to a blank wall. You have personal use of a laptop machine from the 'Laptop for Teachers' scheme, and it is planned that you will have an interactive whiteboard installed in the classroom within six months. How are you going to make most effective use of these facilities?

Much of the work the children undertake will have to be done in at least pairs, although there may well be times when individuals wish to produce some work on the equipment. One of the most important uses of a word processor is its ability to make drafting and redrafting written work a less painful process. One objective for the term would be to ensure that each child actually wrote one piece of their English work on the computer and then printed it out for display. This could be a piece of work that would also allow you to assess their ICT capability. You could decide to choose two children each time, and whatever the piece of written work was, they should write and develop it on the computer. Alternatively, you might expect each child to produce, for example, a book review during the term, and for each one to be written on the computer. You might do this by setting up a basic writing frame for the review so that the actual format of the review sheet always looked the same, and then add each one to a class folder so that they could be encouraged to read through them before choosing their next reading book from the library. In this way there is a real purpose for the activity, with a clearly defined audience.

Adding information to a database on a daily basis gives opportunities for children to be independent in their use of the computer. Set up a very simple database of some easily collectable weather data – most obviously the temperature at the start of the day. Create a rota of pairs of children whose job it is at the beginning of each day to read the temperature of the classroom, and to record it in the class weather database. They should then choose some of the recently collected data and present it in a graphical form together with a sentence of explanation, for display at the front of the school. For example, they might produce a bar chart showing the temperature changes over a period of two weeks. Their description of what the bar chart shows might be 'Every day last week the temperature was at least two degrees colder than it has been any day this week'. In a relatively simple activity, which eventually everyone will be involved in, children will have added data to a database, made a choice of what data to display and the way in which it should be displayed and interpreted what the graph actually shows. They have used the power of the computer to produce a rapid display – a hand-drawn graph by the children would have taken a great deal of time – and then been given an opportunity to interpret some real information. Clearly there is a great deal of scope to make this activity considerably more complex. Add a whole set of data from the school weather station, or get them to compare data from this year with data stored in previous years and to present the comparison graphically, for example.

When the CD-ROM encyclopaedia is in the classroom it does not make obsolete the whole range of reference books that you might well have in the classroom. Set up activities where each group has to find the answers to a series of well structured questions. This could be within the context of many National Curriculum subjects. One group should just use books, while the other just uses CD-ROM encyclopaedias. See which group completes the activity first and then discuss the advantages and disadvantages of the two approaches. Here you are not only developing the children's research skills using two different media, but also giving children the opportunity to evaluate the advantages, as well as the disadvantages, of using an ICT approach.

Again, in an attempt to create more independent learners, encourage children to ask to use the computer at any time when they think that the activity would be enhanced by doing so. The emphasis on them explaining the benefits of using the computer must be strong. You will only agree to them using the computer if you think they have made a good argument.

What theoretical background is there to support the use of ICT?

There is no intention in this book to delve deeply into theories of learning, but a discussion of some of the factors that make working with ICT so effective should be useful.

Vygotsky and the 'zone of proximal development'

Vygotsky, originally writing in Russian in the 1930s, has some very influential insights into the ways in which children learn that have vast implications for children and their use of ICT.

First, there is Vygotsky's idea of the 'zone of proximal development' (ZPD). This is 'the distance between the actual developmental level [of the child] as determined through problem solving and the level of potential development as determined through problem solving under adult guidance or in collaboration with more capable peers' (Vygotsky 1978). Imagine a child is working on a mathematical problem by himself. He has a basic understanding relevant to the mathematics involved, but is finding it difficult to progress. A teacher sees that the child is having problems and intervenes, not by telling him what should be his next step but, through a series of skilfully framed questions, by leading his thinking on from where he is now, to where he needs to be in order to answer the question successfully. 'Oh I see', he says, and successfully completes the problem. There is nothing very outstanding about that particular scenario. It happens a thousand times a day in primary schools throughout the world. But let us explore a little further what is happening in terms of Vygotsky's theory. The child has a grasp of the basic mathematical ideas, but does not understand how to get to the next level of conceptual difficulty, which he needs to do in order to solve the problem. Put simplistically, there is a gap in his understanding between where he is and where he needs to be.

When the teacher comes along and asks the carefully constructed questions, she is supporting his thinking and trying to help him over the gap. In Vygotsky's terms she is providing 'scaffolding'. The 'zone of proximal development' is the size of the gap that can be successfully bridged by the appropriate use of scaffolding. It might be, for example, that the problem the child is working on is much too conceptually difficult, that he will need to go through a whole series of individual stages, each with its own ZPD, and each with a whole series of careful questions from the teacher, and he will need time to consolidate his thinking at each level. Or it might be that the teacher has carefully selected the task in the hope of enabling the child to succeed in developing the enhanced mathematical understanding required in one step.

What implications does this have for ICT? Collaborative work between two or three children in front of a computer working on any type of problem-solving activity can create an environment in which the children within the group can provide the scaffolding that they each need in order to progress. This clearly has implications for the way in which the group is made up, and does not mean that teacher intervention will not be required to ensure that appropriate progress is being made by the whole group.

It also has implications for a child working alone in front of a computer using an integrated learning system or a virtual (or managed) learning environment (these are discussed more fully in Chapter 6). These systems can (although currently do not necessarily) ensure that the questions the child is asked are always at an appropriate level for the capability of the child, and can also take the child forward in carefully measured steps, each equivalent to a ZPD. If a series of straightforward questions are answered quickly and correctly, the management system puts in a more difficult question. The child gets this one wrong, so the computer now provides a short tutorial scaffolding the child's thinking. The child now gets the next three questions right, so the system increases the complexity of the activity still further. This time the child gets the answer right, and does the same with the next four questions of equal complexity. This time there was clearly no need for scaffolding – the child was able to leap across the gap herself. The computer itself is now acting as a very patient tutor, who is permanently available, and is always measuring the understandings of the child. While we should not take away the importance of human intervention, we should not belittle the power that computers now have to manage learning extremely effectively.

Vygotsky's second idea concerns the vital effect that culture and social context have on learning. Again, put simply, learning is a social as well as an individual activity, and what richer environment can there be than a motivating and interactive program to encourage collaborative and meaningful learning between groups of children? Interestingly, then, Vygotsky's ideas can be used to support both children being in control of computers and computers being in control of children.

Howard Gardner and multiple intelligences

In *Frames of Mind: The Theory of Multiple Intelligences*, Howard Gardner (1993) suggested that the traditional measures of intelligence, verbal reasoning tests and mathematics and English, failed to take into account other areas of human endeavour. He originally suggested seven intelligences: kinaesthetic, visual–spatial, mathematical–logical, musical, linguistic, interpersonal and intrapersonal. These were more recently increased to eight by the addition of the naturalist intelligence.

It is probably useful to define these intelligences by describing the attributes that children would demonstrate.

- Linguistic. Children would enjoy reading, telling stories, writing poetry and doing crossword puzzles or word searches.
- Logical–mathematical. Children would enjoy mathematics and science, with interest in strategy games and experiments.
- Musical. Children listen very carefully and often sing to themselves, with an interest in listening to, playing and perhaps composing music.
- Spatial–visual. Children think in images, enjoying drawing, building with construction kits and doing jigsaw puzzles.
- Kinaesthetic. Children like experiencing things through touch and movement, enjoying dance, sport or practical making activities.
- Interpersonal. Children who might well be leaders among their peers, who are good at communicating and can empathise with others.
- Intrapersonal. Children who are self-motivated, are aware of their own feelings, but may be shy.
- Naturalist. Children who specifically have a great interest in the natural world and more generally the ability to recognise, classify and identify patterns.

Each person has access to these intelligences but some are likely to be more developed in one person rather than another. One school in the USA set up the classroom in seven centres where the children worked on a rota basis for approximately two and a half hours each day (Campbell 1989). In the building centre, the children constructed a three-layer replica of the

Earth, using different coloured clays to represent the core, mantle and crust. Then they sliced the sphere in half for the cross-sectional view. In the mathematics centre the children looked at the geometry of circles and in the reading centre they read a book about a group of school children exploring inside the Earth. The music centre allowed the children to listen to music while learning how to spell Earth, crust, mantle and core, and the art centre involved the children cutting out concentric circles of different sizes and colours, and pasting and labelling them to identify the different zones. The working together centre involved children reading a fact sheet and then jointly answering questions. Finally, the personal work centre involved children individually writing about 'Things you would take with you on a journey to the centre of the Earth'. (This work was carried out in 1998, before the eighth intelligence was suggested.)

As Bruce Campbell (1989) comments:

> At the end of the $2^1/_2$ hours spent at the centre, I can say with certainty that every one of my 27 students knew the structure of the earth and perhaps even more importantly, had learned artistically, mathematically, musically, linguistically, kinaesthetically, interpersonally and independently. I have noticed that my role as a teacher dramatically shifts as the students work at their multiple centres. My role becomes that of a facilitator of learning.

This experiment was done without ICT, but we now have the power of multimedia machines that will provide all children with rich sources of information presented in a wide variety of ways. And it will not be long, with the development of Curriculum Online, before it will be possible for children to be able to choose the learning approach they would prefer to use, by selecting an appropriate learning package from within their virtual learning environment rather than it being imposed upon them by the teacher.

It is also worth realising that if a desirable aim is to develop a wide range of intelligences, rather than the limited linguistic and mathematical–logical ones that have long been seen to be important, then children need to be able to work both individually and in groups, they need to communicate and they need to engage in practical activities, including working with materials and dancing and sport, none of which necessitates them using ICT at all and many of which could not be done through the medium of ICT.

When you identify someone who is very able at mathematics, perhaps they will find learning about most things in life much easier if it is done in a logical or mathematical way. You would need to capitalise on this, but also encourage the development of other aspects of the child's thinking. It would appear that the task in hand is enormous, the teacher needing to devise different strategies to focus upon different aspects of intelligence for every area of the curriculum. But that is where the power of multimedia computers may be able to assist. It is feasible that teaching packages could be written focusing on different intelligences. Once we acknowledge that different people learn different things in different ways, and that they can now be encouraged to seek out ways of learning that work for them, the computer has the power to assist in this enormous task. A particular explanation might consist of moving graphic elements, some text and a spoken explanation. Then there might be an interview with a person who was actually there. A whole range of different information in many different forms would allow children to select and make use of the approach they find most appealing.

Isn't ICT just about improved presentation?

Teachers must be aware of the potential of ICT to enable them to prepare and present their teaching more effectively. This is obviously far more than just producing better quality desktop published worksheets. It is vital that the reason for using the particular ICT resource is clearly related to the subject matter that needs to be covered and the learning outcomes of that particular element of work. This has implications at all levels. It is quite easy to select a CD-ROM that has a title the same as the topic that is shortly to be covered and to assume that this will support the children's learning. Without effective evaluation of the material (as discussed in Chapter 4) you will not be certain that the material is either suitable for your audience in terms of reading age or specific content, or in a format that the children will readily be able to access. The work that you wish the children to engage in must be structured to allow the most effective use of the time available.

A further consideration that must be made relates to whether this is the most appropriate way of covering the particular topic anyway. If the school is well resourced with books on the particular topic, and it is a unit of work that has been very successful in previous years, then there may be no justification for using an alternative ICT approach. Or it may be that you will use ICT for a quite small specific element of the work that does something that could not have been done easily without ICT.

At every stage you should be considering if you are using the most appropriate media to meet your teaching objectives. You may, for example, normally talk to the group and hold up some posters to illustrate a particular point. Perhaps you could consider putting together a presentation that includes scanned in images of these posters, and perhaps other images from photographs that would otherwise be too small to show. This could then be displayed on the wall using a digital projector, or on an interactive whiteboard.

The presentation, which could also include interviews with people and music associated with the topic, would supplement and illustrate what you are going to say to the children. But by using a wide range of different media you might well be affecting children whose developed intelligences are not specifically those related to linguistics. Perhaps an interview with someone who lives in a different country, talking about their experiences, could be transmitted over the Internet. This type of material would probably relate well to someone who has a well developed interpersonal intelligence. A description of electricity flowing round a circuit might be very difficult to follow until an animation is produced, so that children are able to relate more closely to a model of the situation, and are helped by the use of concrete ideas about abstract issues. Live information with children talking and colour video inserts of some major current event, picked up from a broadband service such as Espresso, can really bring learning alive in a way that black and white newspaper photographs and text cannot. And the easy way in which data can be transformed instantaneously into graphical representations for thoughtful analysis provides further opportunities for high-order thinking skills to be developed.

Are we concerned with learning or education?

In primary schools there is not a requirement to teach about the ways in which computers work and how they can be programmed, and in some people's definition (and throughout industry and commerce) it is this area of work that is called information technology (IT). What needs to be done in primary schools is to teach children the technical skills to use the computer packages and subsequently teach them how they can use the teaching packages as tools to help them to develop their higher-level thinking skills. The former is the means to an end. The latter is why so much money is being spent on ICT. You are clearly aware of the National Curriculum for ICT as it currently stands. It is about using ICT in an increasingly independent way to find out things, to analyse things and to solve problems. Although the words might change in future incarnations of the document, it is unlikely that the overall philosophy will change. The hardware and software will develop, and there will be new practical ICT skills that will need to be taught, but knowing how to use a computer is useless if you do not know what to use it for.

Make sure you know when and when not to use ICT. A spreadsheet in a science experiment can remove the tedium of repetitive calculations and enable children to focus their attention on the relationship between successive readings. If you have set the spreadsheet up for the group, they might not even be aware of where the numbers in the columns are actually coming from. As long as you are clear what your learning objectives are, this does not have to be a problem. But it is imperative that *you* are clear because the activity as described fails to develop any significant element of numeracy, whereas if the children had filled in a table by hand, using calculators to find the answers, they would have been much more involved, and would probably understand more about the mathematical implications of the activity. Similarly, if the children had set up the spreadsheet themselves, the numeracy element of this activity would have been greatly enhanced. This just serves to illustrate how a simple activity when looked at in considerable detail can cover a very wide range of possible learning outcomes depending on the teaching and learning strategies used.

Because of this it is vital that teachers plan carefully to work out the ways in which ICT will be used to meet teaching and learning objectives in their lessons. Another very important issue is that of appropriate teacher intervention, with teachers identifying key questions that can be used to stimulate and direct pupils' learning.

What strategies can be used to maximise the effectiveness of children's use of ICT?

While the use of ICT can enhance the quality of presentation of the finished product, this can have dangers in that it may mask the poor quality of the content of the work. In an activity that is attempting to consider both ICT and some other subject, the children themselves need to understand that there are two completely different elements to the work. Make sure that children are very clear that the work is actually in two parts (the presentation and the content) and give feedback to the children on the two elements separately. It is amazing how easy it is to be persuaded that a piece of work is of a higher quality than it actually is, just because it is presented in a better way.

There may be times when free exploration is a useful aim, but it should not take place too frequently. The children in school must be given worthwhile learning experiences, and if these are not adequately structured they can spend a great deal of time making very little progress. The biggest time waster may be the Internet. A request to find out something about London on a search engine could find 150,000 separate articles, with the likelihood that many will relate to people's names and consumer products. Very little is to be gained by children having free access to the Internet in this way. But neither is there a great deal to be achieved by giving the child the website you want them to look up (because you have done your homework, and found out that this site contains a great deal of useful information that is relevant to their project). Why do they need to bother to use an expensive communications link to find a site, the information from which you might just as well have printed out and given to each child?

This comes back to the difference between just using ICT and using ICT in appropriate ways. If you want to let them use ICT, then they need to know how to search for information properly, using techniques to eliminate superfluous information. Children therefore need to be taught these techniques, and then they can use them on a search that, you have already identified, will lead to a limited number of useful sites. Increasingly internet service providers (ISPs) will do this for you, and as other organisations provide protected environments (such as Espresso, @school and Grid Club) you will probably find fewer and fewer occasions when it will be necessary to go into the wild, anarchic world that is the Internet.

It is very important that there is progression in the ICT that children undertake, and this is only possible if children are challenged to extend their existing skills. As is discussed in Chapter 4, it is important to highlight children's strengths, but the whole point of an intervention strategy is to get children to analyse what they have done, and to enable them, with support, to go forward.

There has been a great deal of talk about the role of ICT as a tool and how it should be used in the context of all the other subjects of the curriculum. This relates back to the issue of whether we are educating or training children in the use of ICT. This does not mean that you cannot teach children how to use a spreadsheet, because you are not 'allowed' to teach ICT specifically. What it does mean, however, is that the teaching should be as interesting and motivating as any other activity in the primary classroom, and it too should be taught in a context. If you were going to be doing a database activity, where everyone entered their shoe sizes and names into a database and then produced graphs of the results, it would be naive to assume that every child would remember how to use the program based on their previous experience a few months earlier. You would therefore remind them how the database program works, showing them, on a large screen in the classroom, some of the data they used before and some other similar databases, data and graphs that could be produced. You would also be prepared with a basic template that children who were unable to design their own database structure would be able to use. And then you would go into the activity, either with a small group of the class or with a whole group if the school has a computer room.

Are computer games a waste of time?

The definition of a game in the *Collins English Dictionary* is 'an amusement or pastime; a contest with rules, the result being determined by skill, strength or chance'. The first part of the definition indicates why computer games are generally not seen to be an important element of work in school. However, if we refer to the second part of the definition, then there probably is an effective role for such activities in the classroom. In his paper 'Developing children's problem solving', David Whitebread (1997) identifies some of the skills involved in problem-solving:

- understanding and representing the problem;
- gathering and organising information;
- planning and strategies;
- reasoning, hypothesis-testing and decision-making;
- using problem-solving tools.

If an effective strategy could be devised to allow children to develop these skills effectively, then it would seem to be well worth while, and it would appear that playing games, particularly those produced with an educational purpose, actually does develop these skills.

One of the most common problems of teaching and learning is getting children to transfer knowledge and skills from one situation to another, and enabling children to sort out the heart of the problem within a new situation. Most children can answer the question 'What is 25 – 7?', but would find it harder to do the same calculation in a context such as 'If you spend 7p of your 25p pocket money, how much do you have left?'

Children really need practice in sorting out the real nature of the problem, and adventure games can assist here by putting problems into contexts that children find interesting and motivating. Adventure games usually require you to gather together information from various 'locations' and to bring it all together at the end of the game. You do not get far in many adventure games unless you devise a plan. Many encourage children to draw a 'map' of the game, so that they are able to have a two-dimensional (or in more complex games a three-dimensionsal) representation of the game on paper. This assists you in devising further strategies. Some programs will also benefit greatly from taking notes, and this is the very type of program that benefits so much from being undertaken in a group where cooperation and discussion can lead to considerable language development and collaboration.

As with all software, it is important that you think carefully about the content of the adventure game. Are you happy that you are using a piece of motivating software that encourages collaborative and problem-solving approaches to learning, but has a content that does not relate at all to any other work that is being done, or does not even have links to any National Curriculum work? Would the activity be much more worthwhile if the content was equally as relevant as the approach? It probably depends on the amount of time you intend to devote to the activity.

How should I use a computer in the classroom?

In her paper 'Classroom investigations: exploring and evaluating how IT can support learning', Bridget Somekh (1997) identifies three approaches that teachers can take when using computers.

Some view the computer as a tutor, with the expectation that a child will sit down in front of the machine and be 'taught' by it, with no further intervention from the teacher until the work is finished. Others view the computer as a neutral tool, in that children will be able to use it to complete tasks that they will have originally done with a pen and pencil. The task will not have changed, but the tool will have. Teachers with this view are likely to concentrate on the presentational benefits that a computer can provide. The third group see the computer as a cognitive tool that can be used to enhance children's learning by allowing them to do things that are only realistically possible using a computer. Here we can include activities such as drafting and redrafting on screen, analysing graphical representations of measurements made by remote sensors and communicating by e-mail with children from across the globe.

Like most simple classifications, this provides a useful model, but it would be wrong to assume that any one view is the one and only correct approach. In your reading of this book, my hope is that you will see the immense power of the computer as a cognitive tool, but increasingly children will use the computer as a tutor, using integrated learning systems, virtual learning environments or other less sophisticated packages, and it would be naive to suppose that teachers and children will not want to use the computer to desktop publish posters and worksheets, when previously they would have used pencils, felt-tip pens and typewriters. What is probably most important is that in your planning you realise that there are at least three distinct ways of using a computer and that you clearly identify the role that it is playing in each particular activity. It is quite likely that as you are getting children to learn how to use a computer they are likely to be involved in more activities that use the computer as a neutral tool, but subsequently, as they become more independent and more capable in their ICT skills and techniques, the role of the computer as a cognitive tool should increase considerably.

What are some of the higher-order skills?

Evaluating information is an important element of ICT, in particular as it relates to the Internet. Previously, when children used books or television programmes as their sources of information, you were clear that they were produced by organisations that had checked most of the information. As soon as you use material from the Internet, you need to explain to children that they need to think very carefully about its accuracy, validity, reliability, plausibility and bias. Anyone can set up a website, and there is nothing to say that any of the information on it is true. With primary age children, it is probably best not to let them have a free rein on the Internet, but it is worthwhile introducing them to the idea that just because it is on a computer screen, it is not necessarily correct. The most useful strategy for children of this age to use is to explore a number of sources, and to compare the information in each. Only when you receive the same information from each should you start to believe it. Children should therefore be encouraged always to explore alternatives, rather than being satisfied with their first effort.

Other higher-order skills include modelling numeric relationships, which can be done very effectively using a spreadsheet, and analysing what causes particular changes to occur. There is also a great deal of work that can be done in predicting patterns and rules, recognising patterns and hypothesising, particularly in work related to science.

What is the impact of ICT on everyday applications?

It is important that children are made aware that ICT is all around us, and is likely to be an important element of their lives. In some ways, this is more important for adults, many of whom are not familiar with ICT, rather than children who have grown up with it as a normal part of their lives. A few years ago I bought a new microwave oven. As is now commonplace, it had membrane switches and an alphanumeric display. It also had a feature that would cook certain items automatically just by pressing the appropriate button. I decided to try it out with seven jacket potatoes. I was momentarily mesmerised by the display, which read '7 Jacket Potatoes'. This microwave can count potatoes! After a few moments I realised that '7' was in fact the program number, but I had been prepared to believe that the oven was capable of counting them. Children would not have had any problems with that situation, as they probably would have no reason to believe that a microwave could not count potatoes! So perhaps this is why we need to provide opportunities to talk with children about what computers can and cannot do. They need to be fully aware of what ICT is good at, and what it is unable to do.

Let us take an example of an 'expert system' that is gradually beginning to emerge. There are now computer systems that can ask a series of questions and then, as a result of your responses, provide a diagnosis of what illness you are suffering from. It is suggested that it could be operated by a nurse, and would provide 'out-of-hours' cover, to avoid doctors having to go out on so many visits. What is your reaction to this? Positive or negative? Most of the newspaper reports were certainly negative, but think about it logically. The computer is doing nothing more than asking a series of hierarchically structured questions, and making a decision as to which question to ask next, based on the previous answer. The questions are the same ones that the doctor would ask, and you would have no worry that the computer missed one out by mistake. If the doctor was there she would also be able to see the patient and to examine him, getting valuable extra data on which to base her diagnosis, but as a method of telephone screening, isn't this just as good a method as a doctor asking these questions over the phone to ascertain if a visit is necessary?

It is this type of discussion that children of all ages need to be involved in, so that they realise that computers are not taking over the world, but are being used to assist people in everyday tasks. We are not going to see an intelligent computer – yet.

How can I manage ICT in the classroom?

As in most aspects of classroom management, there is not just one approach, but part of the skill is selecting the right approach to achieve the appropriate learning outcomes, bearing in mind the restrictions you might have in terms of both hardware and software. Let us consider a number of possible approaches.

One large screen – whole class

Inevitably there are going to be times when you want to show children how to use a particular element of a piece of software, to discuss the findings of some data analysis, to share the information found from a particular website or perhaps to round up a lesson by doing a quick search on a CD-ROM to find the answer to a question that cropped up during the morning. Interactive whiteboards, or at least ceiling-mounted digital projectors, are now commonly installed in primary school classrooms. This allows for high-quality whole-class teaching to take place, giving opportunities for exciting and stimulating starter and plenary activities to be carried out.

Many teachers produce their own resources for these facilities, usually based around Microsoft PowerPoint, but as a result of the Curriculum Online initiative resource developers are producing true digital content designed specifically for teacher use. One such product is PrimaryViewPoint, which provides PowerPoint presentations for each of the units of the QCA science scheme of work. Incorporating many high-quality photographs and animations, it provides an ideal backdrop for the teacher's explanations. As it is developed in PowerPoint it also allows teachers to edit the material so that it can be matched to suit the children in your own class. It is true digital content in that it has been produced specifically for whole-class teaching, with photographs, animations and text being of an appropriate size for projecting on to a screen. Beware of much material currently available on the Curriculum Online website, which is merely material originally produced for the printed page that has been transferred to the screen, with the inherent problems of text size and fitness for purpose.

Small groups or pairs – part of class

Given the existing ICT provision in many schools, this is likely to be the situation that needs to be managed. The classroom contains a number of computers, but insufficient for anything like the whole class to be engaged on ICT activity. This is where you need a very precise programme and record-keeping system so that you can keep a clear overview of the progress that each child is making. One issue to consider is the make-up of each group, which should not be left to chance, but should be carefully managed depending upon the nature of the activity. Sometimes you may want an element of peer tutoring, at other times you may prefer children of similar abilities working together and at yet other times you might want to organise the groups carefully so that they contain children who have different skills to contribute to the specific activity. Another vital element is that your intervention should be an important part of your planning for the activity. You must devise an activity for the rest of the group that

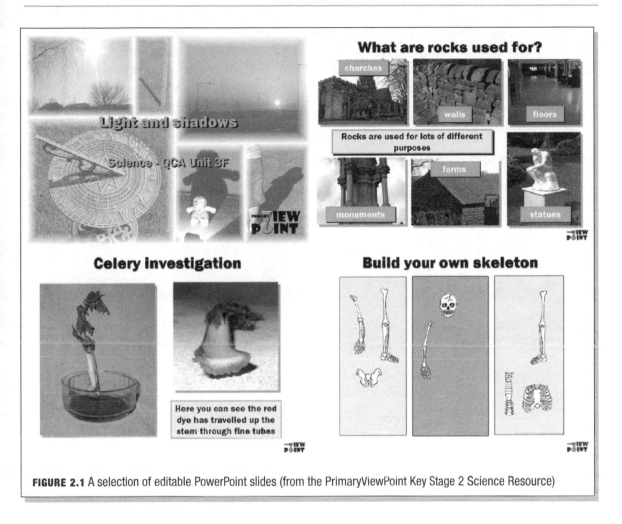

FIGURE 2.1 A selection of editable PowerPoint slides (from the PrimaryViewPoint Key Stage 2 Science Resource)

will give you opportunities to discuss the ICT work with the children on the computer. By leaving them to get on with their work solely by themselves, you will not encourage them to develop and extend their existing ICT skills.

Small groups or pairs – whole class

This is the situation you will find yourself in if your school has a room or corridor with a substantial number of computers together in one place. The whole class will be able to engage in similar collaborative activities. This approach will encourage discussion and teamwork and the teacher will spend the time intervening to ensure that each group is making effective progress.

Individuals – whole class

This will be the model if your school uses integrated learning systems or virtual learning environments, where children normally work individually, perhaps using headphones. The computer is very much in control of the child's learning and it is very difficult for a teacher to intervene. It also requires enormous expenditure, in terms of both hardware and software, to enable the whole class to be working on their own computers at the same time. This is unlikely to be a situation that many schools will find themselves in, and it may not even be desirable, in terms of the lack of opportunity for teacher intervention.

Main teaching and learning issues

- Slight changes to teaching strategy can radically alter learning outcomes.

- Not all work undertaken at a computer will develop children's ICT capability.

- Make sure you know how you are using the computer in the classroom – as a tutor, a neutral tool or a cognitive tool.

- Wherever possible use it to do something that without ICT would be difficult or impossible.

The Management of ICT in the Primary School

This chapter looks at all the management issues related to ICT in the primary school. Many of these will need to be discussed in the school's ICT policy document and development plan. The school's ICT coordinator plays a vital role in the successful integration of ICT into the curriculum, and it is hoped that he or she will find the questions and answers in this chapter of particular use.

What is the role of the ICT coordinator?

When you start to consider the multifarious roles of the coordinator, you may wonder when she or he has time to teach. Many will be responsible for all the hardware and software on the school site. Increasingly this is seen as an inappropriate role for an experienced professional educator and many primary schools are seeing the value of purchasing technical support. In many cases this will not be a full-time appointment, but will involve buying into a local education authority (LEA) technical support service, or a group of schools sharing the costs of a full time technician.

It is important that coordinators keep up-to-date with new developments, and disseminate this information as appropriate. They are also likely to be the first point of contact for LEA or other ICT advisory teams, and are likely to attend courses and attempt to get the school involved in relevant projects, competitions and award schemes.

An important issue to consider is how many tasks the coordinator actually has to do, compared with how many she is responsible for. Although many job descriptions identify work on software, hardware and training, for example, there may be a case for splitting the tasks between those she will actual undertake and those she will oversee. Value for money is an issue here, and it is doubtful whether a fully trained teacher is the most appropriate person to spend all day fixing jammed printers.

Perhaps the most important role is in producing the school ICT policy document and ICT strategic action plan, and subsequently ensuring that it is carried out. Once you are happy that all the paperwork and systems are in place you might like to consider applying for the NAACEmark Quality ICT in Schools award (www.naace.org). This is a national award that recognises a school's success in developing and implementing a strategic approach to ICT. The aim of the NAACEmark for ICT in schools is to

- promote the importance of ICT to the curriculum;
- improve the effective use of ICT in teaching and learning;
- promote quality provision in the teaching of ICT;
- improve the use of ICT as a management tool to enhance provision and communication;
- disseminate good practice.

The important thing to realise is that the NAACEmark just recognises something that you need to do anyway. It is not intended that a great deal of extra work is necessary in order to achieve the NAACEmark successfully.

How do I write an ICT policy?

There might well be a temptation to find an ICT policy from another school and change the name, so that the job is finished – the so-called 'Tipp-Ex policy'! This does not, however, produce a very useful document. The production of a policy is not just a chore but a vital element in the way in which your school delivers ICT.

A useful overriding thought should be that this document will provide students and new members of staff with assistance for their planning and delivery of ICT. You must clearly assume that everyone also has access to the relevant National Curriculum documentation, and so the policy does not need to replicate that, but it does need to highlight the particular way in which the school feels that it should deliver this aspect of the curriculum.

A good way to start thinking about the policy is to ask yourself what you would have liked to have known about ICT when you first started working at the school.

How do I involve all the staff?

All staff should clearly be involved in a discussion leading to the production of a new ICT policy. However, it will be your task to expedite the process. Arranging a series of full staff meetings where you hope to produce a policy from a blank sheet of paper is not an effective way of using people's time. Conversely, a policy that you write and present as a *fait accompli* will not have the support of many of the staff, and will not have benefited from a range of perspectives through which a policy needs to have gone.

A compromise would be the production of an outline draft that is given to all members of staff, and on which they would be asked for comments. Form a small working group to discuss the various inputs and to produce a more substantial draft. This document should then be made available to all staff, together with a list of features about which the group requests some advice. This could then form the basis of a whole-staff discussion. The working group then finalises the policy for presentation to the head and governors (if they have not already been heavily involved in its development).

What should I include in the introduction?

You should include something about the nature of ICT that the school is happy with. For example, you may decide that ICT is going to be extremely high profile in your school, and you are going to be at the cutting edge of developments in the field. You are involved in many national initiatives, and see ICT as a way of enhancing literacy and numeracy for all the children in your school. This will immediately identify to anyone reading the policy that ICT is an integral part of education in the school, and the rest of the document will inform them how it is achieved. If your aspirations are not quite as extensive then this should also be made clear in the introduction.

You should next identify the audience for the policy, most often the staff of the school, the governors, parents, students on teaching practice, officers of the LEA or other funding bodies and other visitors such as Ofsted. The policy should be there to provide the vision and framework for all the ICT developments in the school. The policy should be clear as to how the school views ICT now, and what it is striving for in the future. This section should also cover the methodology of policy formulation, identifying who was involved and how frequently it is to be reviewed. The ICT policy should clearly be linked to the school development plan and cross-referenced to other policy documents produced by the school.

What elements of ICT should the policy cover?

Your policy may include the whole school's use of ICT, including the strategies to enable staff to develop their own ICT capability and the ways in which ICT is or will be used to improve the management of the school. How, for example, are you going to encourage staff to make more use of ICT? Some staff may already have computers at home, so perhaps the schools could contribute to an Internet service provider (ISP) so that they can use their own computers to search for appropriate information for forthcoming projects. Perhaps the school will purchase two multimedia notebooks that staff can borrow for evenings and weekends. Perhaps the school will negotiate with a computer supplier to provide discounts on purchases that teachers make. The evidence from a number of projects suggested, not surprisingly, that if teachers are given high-quality portable computers they use them, and as a result are in a much better position to evaluate the ways in which ICT can influence teaching and learning for the benefit of children. This led to the national Laptops for Teachers scheme, where teachers in schools are given laptops funded from government grants. These should be given to teachers as their own professional tools, to keep with them until they leave the school.

Is the coordination role one that encompasses both curriculum use and management use of ICT?

In most cases currently this is probably not the case, but as the links between management and curriculum ICT develop, in such areas as assessment, reporting to parents and assessment through the school's management information system (MIS), this may be something worth considering. Increasingly, data is being made available that can inform future practice, and many management information systems assist in the analysis of value-added data.

What national, local and internal factors influence the school's aims for ICT?

Clearly there is currently a national imperative for the use of ICT in schools, with the central government initiatives of Curriculum Online, broadband developments and the ICT in Schools section of the DfES. Similarly, the NOF ICT training programme should have moved all staff in the school forward and there are new opportunities for CPD programmes that focus specifically on how ICT can be used to enhance subject teaching.

These initiatives clearly impinge on your own policy to a greater or lesser extent. If you, as a school, were already very well resourced with ICT-capable staff and a good range of skills among the children, then the national factors will confirm what you, as a school, had already decided, and will allow you to work towards being a centre of excellence in your particular area. If, however, your school is currently not well resourced, and teachers need considerable training in ICT, then the national factors will probably have a higher profile in your particular policy. This background information will then allow you to produce a clear statement of aims for your school in its use of ICT.

How is ICT organised within the curriculum?

We are now getting down to the detail of the way in which ICT is used within the school. This should be not a 'wish list' but a realistic expectation based on the resources and skills that are currently available. There are other places within the policy where possibilities for the future can be addressed, and when these are actively taking place in schools then practice has developed and the policy should be revised to take that into account.

This is also a good time to identify how the school will deliver National Curriculum ICT requirements, as well as how it will use ICT to assess or manage the learning process. Remember, these are two very different aspects of ICT use in school.

Very important principles can be addressed in this section. For example, does the school give opportunities for some older children to choose to use computer applications for particular tasks because they believe it will make the task easier or more effective. If it does, the teachers need to know how important this independent work is seen to be, and they also need to be aware of the organisational strategies that are set up to make it possible. The school may also have invested heavily in an integrated learning system as part of its numeracy drive. Teachers need to know that they are expected to use it with their children, and new staff will also be expected to attend training sessions on its effective use.

It is almost certain that ICT will be an important element of long- and medium-term planning, and the policy needs to state how teachers are involved in this process. As the amount of hardware in school increases and there are obvious increased pressures to use it extensively, strategic planning becomes increasingly important. While it is relatively easy to organise the use of one computer in your own room, where there are no constraints, it requires much more planning to use a network room including 16 machines with Internet access and interactive whiteboard if the facilities are to provide value for money.

The medium- and long-term planning is clearly vital in terms of progression of ICT skills. In any cross-curricular activity making use of ICT it is likely that you are looking not only at developing ICT capability, but also at covering some element of other National Curriculum subjects. A simple example would be word-processing a letter, covering writing and the concept of it being written in a particular style for a specific audience. As set out here it could be an activity suitable for a five-year-old or a twenty- or fifty-five-year-old. However, as one matures one would expect to see maturity in the style of the letter and a closer match between the style of the writing and the recipient of the letter. What changes, however, would you expect to see in the ICT capability shown? Perhaps a use of *tab* keys rather than space bar, and the use of *line wrap*, rather than hard returns, but these are not significant developments in knowledge. Progression in ICT skills will undoubtedly mean using more sophisticated features and a wider range of programs. This does not mean that a child who is competent in using a word processor should not use it for writing a letter, but it should be acknowledged that the computer is now being used as a tool, to do a particular task. It should be compared with a child using a pen to write a story. The focus on the activity is making up the story, and there is not a thought in the teacher's mind that it is also developing their pen manipulation skills. It is therefore important that children are given real opportunities to develop and extend their own ICT capability through challenging activities designed to make use of more sophisticated features.

There also need to be clear guidelines on planning for differentiation. This is increasingly important, as the home ownership of computers continues to rise at an extremely rapid rate. At its most fundamental it is quite possible that children in your school will have faster machines with more sophisticated software at home than is available in the school itself. Imagine the demotivating effect of a child using a very basic word-processing package with a mouse that does not work, when at home he or she could produce a piece of work that was many times more attractive, and in a fraction of the time. Or a child is dissatisfied with the amount of information that she can find on a particular topic in the school library, when she knows that within a few minutes on her Internet connection at home she would be able to download a great deal of useful and relevant information. The school must have a policy for dealing with this. Presumably, it should encourage children to make use of the equipment that they have access to, at the same time ensuring that the school rapidly obtains equivalent resources, so that children who do not have such home-based facilities are not significantly disadvantaged. Making these facilities available as part of homework clubs would also be a useful strategy.

What teaching and learning styles are required for ICT?

The reason why so much money has been and is going to be invested in ICT is that it is believed to enhance teaching and learning. The school policy should therefore make it clear in what ways this is going to be done. Although these issues are discussed in more detail in

Chapter 2, making the child more autonomous and providing interactive and motivating activities that make use of real-life information really need to be identified here. What learning styles are you able to support? What teaching styles do you encourage? How do you differentiate between learners and ensure that they are all challenged?

What sort of access do staff and children have to ICT equipment?

When so much capital is tied up with the school's computers, there is obviously an underlying feeling that they should be in use for a great deal of the time. The policy should therefore identify how and when the equipment can be used. Increasingly, schools will have computer networks, with the computers being either grouped together in one or two rooms, or distributed throughout the classrooms. There will also be opportunities for portable computers to be used by children, and we are rapidly getting to the stage where it would not be unreasonable for a primary school to have a class set of 30 portable computers. Indeed, it is only a little further into the future that we can expect each child to have his or her own. Currently, the smaller notebook and palmtop computers are only able to run the normal business applications, and some of these may not be particularly effective on small screens (I am thinking particularly of presentation software), so there are going to be many applications still for the desktop machine with a large colour monitor.

You will probably want children to be able to use computers outside the normal lesson time. This is probably easier to manage and supervise if all the computers are together in one room. A number of schools have computers situated in wide communal carpeted corridors, which allows easy access for children who suddenly decide that they would like to use a particular piece of software.

As hardware becomes cheaper, it may be feasible to have some portable or palmtop machines for loan, so that children can borrow them to complete work at home. This will assist in the equal opportunities issue related to children who have computers at home.

What equal opportunities issues are there?

The policy needs to state how the school ensures that all children have opportunities to use ICT according to their particular needs. The groups of children that need to be considered particularly would be those with English as a second language and those with particular special educational needs (see Chapter 10). You also need to have strategies to ensure that gender stereotypes are not promulgated (boys always monopolising computer equipment), and that the home provision of ICT, or lack of it, is taken into account by the school.

Do I need to include details of assessment of children's progress?

In your policy you need to make a distinction between what use the school will make of computers for the administration of assessment across the whole school curriculum, and how you will assess and report on children's ICT capability.

If you are going to use ICT extensively for record keeping and such like, then that should be covered comprehensively in this section. Issues of assessment and reporting, as they relate to ICT, can probably best be cross-referenced to the school's assessment policy (see Chapter 4 for details).

How are the physical resources to be managed?

As the amount of computer equipment in schools rapidly increases, greater attention needs to be paid to its actual management. With one computer in every classroom, it probably was reasonable to delegate the responsibility for the equipment to each class teacher. They are trained in basic housekeeping tasks, and they come to the ICT coordinator for assistance when required. But when schools contain networks of computers, all linked to one main server, and some of the machines are in a room of their own, other strategies will need to be devised.

One strategy worth considering is employing someone to manage the computer system in the school (I repeat this even though a reviewer of an earlier edition of this book suggested that I was being unrealistic in this suggestion). For an ICT coordinator, it is not always clear to others how much of your time is spent doing extremely basic 'fire fighting' activities such as freeing jammed printers, or recovering a 'lost' piece of work by closing down a few windows that were covering it up. At one school, when the ICT coordinator left, the headteacher decided to take over the role, as all other staff already had considerable coordinating responsibilities. Within three weeks the school was advertising for a part-time ICT technician. Ongoing costs certainly have to be considered, but these should be considered in the context of both the total expenditure on ICT equipment, which is obviously rising, and the cost of a fully qualified teacher's time, compared with that of a part-time technician. The one danger in this approach is that teachers could assume no responsibility for maintaining and keeping up-to-date with computer software, but this can be alleviated if part of the role of the ICT technician is seen as training staff effectively to solve problems. A technician should have that little more time to train staff in how to repair a printer, whereas the ICT coordinator would only find the time to repair it themselves, meaning that the teacher will have to rely on their assistance the next time, and the next time. A little extra time spent early on will definitely repay itself many times over in the fullness of time.

In the days when a school had few computers, issues of their management were not very high on the agenda. Now that almost all schools will have considerable capital expenditure tied up in hardware and software, management of the resource is extremely important. The policy should state how the computers are distributed around the school, the rationale for this distribution and the software that is available on each machine. It is probably sensible to put this detailed information in the form of an appendix, so that it can be easily changed and updated as appropriate.

There should be clear procedures for repair and maintenance, and the school really needs to consider a maintenance contract with either an LEA or another support agency. If your curriculum is increasingly built upon an ICT framework, then it will quickly fail if one or two computers break down. Leasing computers is an approach that will have built-in mainte-nance, although it is a more expensive solution in the long run than buying outright. Make it clear who is informed when a repair is requested.

The policy should also make it clear how the budget is determined. A sensible strategy to have is based on the requirements of the school development plan, which will have been approved by the governing body. A typical scenario might be that the ICT coordinator is asked to put forward proposals based on a recent Ofsted inspection. These should include not only costings for more machines and software, but also a rationale for the request in terms of enhanced teaching and learning for the children. It is also a good idea to set out a long-term view, perhaps five years, so that the vision can be identified, and to identify that computers have a finite useful life – which is probably currently four or five years.

It is also useful to make clear the process by which new software can be purchased. A new teacher coming to the school who has had considerable success with a particular package may well extol its virtues, and it is important that this broadening of experience is encouraged. It is, however, useful if some meetings are arranged where groups of teachers look at and eval-uate prospective software purchases. Wherever possible, someone on the staff should evaluate the software, because demonstrations by firms themselves are often very slick and give the impression that everything is possible. Only when you try it yourself can you really see the limitations. When teachers request specific pieces of software, encourage them to iden-tify the main advantages of such a piece of software over the package that currently exists. It is unwise to proliferate, say, the number of word-processing packages that children have access to unless there are very good reasons for doing so. In terms of manageability, it is prob-ably better if all machines have a common range of software on them, which children and staff become familiar with.

Installing software is a very time-consuming business. One of the advantages of a network system is that the software is installed once, and each computer then loads it down from the main server. This also has the advantage that all machines have access to the same library of software.

Many computer systems have front ends that are designed to give certain groups of chil-dren access to a limited range of software, or particular places to store their files. You need to decide who has access to this password-protected system. It may be too draconian to say that only the ICT coordinator can change configurations of machines, but then it is also very time-consuming to reconfigure after an error has been made. Whichever approach you go for, make it clear in the policy and stick to it.

What health and safety issues do I need to consider?

Generally, in primary schools, children do not spend sufficient time in front of a computer screen to warrant undue concern. However, as teaching styles evolve that imply more exten-sive use of computers, health and safety issues will need to be taken more seriously. Children need to maintain a correct posture when working on a computer, and this means sitting on a chair that is of a suitable height (in a school situation, this might imply variable height chairs), with a monitor generally at eye level, and with plenty of room to work with both a keyboard and a mouse. Eye strain is another issue, and it may be worthwhile gradually building up a stock of anti-glare screens, which fix to the front of monitors, to prevent this. Alternatively, for new purchases you may consider flat screens, which cause far fewer eye strain problems.

Clearly, as with all other electrical equipment in school, it should be checked regularly by a qualified technician or electrician. Trailing mains leads and extension cables leading from the one socket in the classroom can cause serious hazards, and consideration must be given to installing additional power points to avoid these. Similar care must also be taken with the other leads that are inevitably linked to computers, such as those of keyboards, printers and scanners. Many of these problems can be easily overcome if you plan for your computers to be in fixed locations. It is more difficult, however, if your computers are mobile, either because you want to use them in a number of classrooms or because you need to move them into secure areas at the end of each day.

How should the policy be monitored?

There is no point having a policy if there is no clear strategy to see if it is actually being carried out in the school. It will probably be the ICT coordinator's role, perhaps delegated to year coordinators, to see that the teaching, planning, assessment and use of ICT are carried out according to the policy. These are clearly issues that will be discussed at year and whole-school planning meetings. It would probably be useful if there were occasional monitoring exercises carried out by senior management to observe practice within the school to ensure that it matches with both the policy and the long- and medium-term planning. There clearly should also be a way of monitoring staff development to ensure that staff needs are clearly identified and that in-service provision satisfactorily satisfies those needs. It would be useful to mention any needs analysis instruments that you might use in order to identify staff training needs.

Because of the speed of technological advances and governmental initiatives in this field an ICT policy is inevitably going to evolve quite rapidly, and it probably needs to be reviewed at least every two years, and perhaps even annually.

What are the legal issues I should consider?

Copyright

It is vital that software is appropriately licensed and purchased, and you should be aware that you do not actually have to sell pirate copies of software to be breaking the law. Buying from reputable dealers is probably the best way of ensuring you do not encounter illegal software. The legal penalties for infringement are considerable, including unlimited fines and up to two years in prison.

Shareware gives you an opportunity to try software out for a period before you purchase it. This often comes on the cover disks of the numerous computer magazines that are available each month. In this field as in so many others you may be subject to software overload. Do you really have time to download and evaluate all the megabytes of software that one of these CD-ROMs offers. Increasingly you will be able to download software off the Internet. Currently this is mainly cut-down demonstration material or beta versions of software (software that the company is asking you to try out before it is put on sale). This should be seen as an improvement, as not so long ago the first versions of many programs were so full of 'bugs' that you were often sent complete upgrades free of charge. If we were expected to buy cars in this way we would have something to say about it.

Often software comes 'bundled' together with a machine. With many education suppliers this is often a carefully constructed package ensuring that you have a wide range of software applications appropriate to the age of the children. Software bundles from other suppliers may not be so educationally relevant, and may, for example, have a different 'office' suite included. This means you will have to suffer the incompatibility problems, or buy another office suite for your new machine. You may be better off buying a machine with limited software and installing it to your own specific requirements. Remember that with bundled software you may not get the normal full documentation – and in many cases you will not get anything. You will have either to rely on the help files, or to purchase one of the enormous software handbooks that are available, typically costing between £30 and £40.

Freeware, as its name suggests, is free. There may well be a few small interesting pieces of freeware available, but there is unlikely to be anything of a substantial nature.

If you are in doubt about any software copyright issue you should get in touch with the Federation Against Software Theft (FAST) for further information.

Defamation

This will be an important issue when children in your school are able to publish their own work on the Internet, or send e-mails that can be read by large numbers of people. There needs to be a procedure in place to ensure that all material appearing on the school's website is approved before it 'goes live'. It would probably be unwise to give children the password to allow them to edit the school's website. This should probably be done by a nominated member of staff, often known as 'The Webmaster'.

Unless you are happy that a particular discussion group is of great educational use, they are probably best avoided by primary age children. Although software is available that will censor both incoming and outgoing messages for bad language, you are not in a position to know who is involved in the discussion, and what their ulterior motive may be. Individual e-mail links with known schools are probably much easier to police, and more useful educationally. Any defamation in these circumstances could be dealt with in the same way that the school would deal with graffiti or the passing of derogatory notes around the classroom.

Data protection

The Data Protection Act requires that personal information about people should be obtained and processed in a fair and lawful way. It should also be appropriate in terms of the purpose for which it is required. It clearly has to be accurate, and this means that it needs to be kept up-to-date. It should also not be retained for longer than necessary for the particular purpose for which it is held. It is an important element of the law that anyone is entitled to be told if any personal data is held about them, that they are able to see it, and if necessary they can have the information corrected or erased. This has to be done at reasonable intervals and without undue delay or expense.

Organisations that hold data have to take appropriate security measures to ensure that others do not gain unauthorised access, which might result in disclosure, alteration or deletion. Accidental loss or destruction must also be avoided.

One interesting feature of the law is that it does allow for data collected to be used for historical, statistical or research purposes even though that was not the initial purpose for the data collection, as long as no harm or distress is likely to be caused to individuals.

In the context of a primary school, the school's management software is in place to record relevant data about the children, and perhaps staff, in the school. All details, such as names, addresses and contact numbers, are clearly important and relevant information. So too are the marks and assessment scores, which are intended to inform the parents anyway, and so will be readily available to them.

Censorship

This is going to be an increasingly important issue as more schools make use of Internet connections and therefore are able to access a whole world of information, some of which may be most undesirable. Currently Internet service providers that specialise in education filter out sites that are deemed undesirable, so that no one is able to gain access to them.

Commercial Internet service providers do not have such services, but there is software that you load on to your own machine that you can use to delete or restrict access to undesirable sites. Most of these programs are not very sophisticated in the way in which they work. They scan the text of all material downloading from the Internet, and any words that match a list of undesirable words included within the software are blanked out.

Some of the software comes with default lists of words, and others allow you to make up your own. I have always contemplated what the staff meeting would be like at which the school's list of forbidden words was drawn up. There are clearly concerns from some groups that this very coarse level of filtering is likely to restrict access to some worthwhile material.

It is also important that the school has an acceptable use policy (AUP) to formalise the ways in which the ICT facilities can and cannot be used in school. The document needs to balance the ability to exploit the educational potential of Internet resources with appropriate safeguards against unacceptable activity.

The Superhighways Safety Site (http://safety.ngfl.gov.uk/schools) contains a lot of useful information on this topic. One of the documents available on the site is entitled 'Developing an acceptable use policy'. This identifies what an acceptable use policy might include:

- a requirement that all potential users of the Internet understand basic conventions and navigation techniques before going on line and accessing web pages;

- information reminding children that logs are kept of sites visited and why;

- an undertaking by users to act responsibly and use the Internet in school for course-related work only;

- an undertaking by children to respect copyright and not to plagiarise others' work;

- an agreement by users to download pages to personal floppy disks, rather than to the machine's hard disk, and an explanation of why such restrictions are necessary;

- permission for members of staff to check personal disks for viruses and unsuitable material;

- a pledge by users not to attempt to access unsuitable material;

- a reminder that the possession of certain types of unsuitable material can lead to prosecution by the police;

- information on sanctions for violations of the agreed acceptable use policy.

Access to chat rooms is almost certainly banned by your Internet service provider. There is very little to be gained by children using these types of facilities. An exception should be made for websites such as 'Grid Club', which provide moderated discussion groups on a range of relevant issues in a very safe environment.

There might be times when you want to include photographs of children on a school website, but avoid the use of the first name and surname of individuals in a photograph. This reduces the risk of inappropriate, unsolicited attention from people outside the school. A useful rule to remember is 'If the child is named, avoid using their photograph – if the photograph is used, avoid naming the child'. Asking for parental permission to use an image of a child ensures that parents are aware of the way the image of their child is representing the school.

How can I evaluate and become more familiar with software?

Evaluating software can be a very time-consuming activity. Written material can be evaluated quite informally. An initial skim through can be followed by a more detailed look at more particular issues, such as the nature of illustrations, language level, accessibility and the way in which the material is organised.

In content-rich software, an effective evaluation can take a great deal of time specifically because it is not written in a linear format. You therefore need to work out the navigational features and try to explore as much of the content as you can – not an easy task. The website Curriculum Online (www.curriculumonline.gov.uk) plans to provide detailed independent evaluations of all the products that are available for purchase with e-learning credits. However you do it, you need to evaluate how effective the material is at meeting the teaching objectives that you have set and to judge its suitability for the children's age, prior experience, language level and social and cultural background.

There are many software checklists that are available, but a useful in-service activity, prior to undertaking software evaluation yourself, may well be to develop one of your own, using samples that you have picked up from a wide range of sources. You might decide to give numerical gradings to different elements of the program, or you may prefer to go for a more holistic qualitative approach, writing down general descriptions of each element of the software. A useful strategy would be to set aside one half of a training day for teachers within a school to evaluate new programs for the forthcoming year. In pairs, teachers could perhaps evaluate two packages in detail, and provide feedback on their findings to the rest of the group during the latter part of the morning. This would ensure that all the staff became familiar with what was available before the whole-school planning meetings took place.

Categories that should be considered for comment include content, how long it has been published, suitability for National Curriculum coverage, reading age, ease of use, the presentation of the material and the features that it has available.

Let us look at an example of the type of evaluation that could be written on an imaginary piece of software.

The information provided is clear, but it is basically text-based, and there are American spellings. There are some good photographs, but no sound, animation or video. It was published two years ago, and there has been a further edition since. The reading age is appropriate for Year 4 and Year 5 children, and the material matches very well with a National Curriculum geography topic. The navigation from page to page is by clear and simple 'cassette tape recorder type' interface. All the text and pictures can be selected and pasted into other applications, but the 'copyright' tags cannot be edited out. In order to use this effectively children will need to use simple 'AND' searches to find more specific information. There are a number of 'game' type applications as part of the package, two of which are useful, and two of which would not develop children's learning in this topic. They cannot be disabled. If children were given a series of clearly structured tasks, then they could develop their searching strategies in the context of a geographical topic by using this package. We do, however, have class sets of books that cover this material in a very similar way, so we might be better letting children develop their searching skills using a CD-ROM with more multimedia elements.

How can I use the Internet for my own professional development?

Increasingly the Internet can provide teachers with a great deal of information that is extremely relevant to their professional work. All the major organisations concerned with ICT and education have websites with resources and the ability to discuss with other professionals issues that affect you.

Here is a list of the main websites that are concerned with ICT education.

- Department for Education and Skills (www.dfes.gov.uk). This is a general information site about all things related to education policy. It incorporates the Standards Site, which includes the QCA Schemes of Work.

- British Educational Communications and Technology Agency (www.becta.org.uk). This is an organisation whose role is to try out new ideas about using ICT in education, evaluate them and disseminate good practice to all schools. Its ICT Advice website is an excellent starting point if you want find out what is happening in the field of ICT. It links with subject associations to develop good practice in using ICT to enhance teaching and learning in all subjects.

- The National College of School Leadership (www.ncsl.org.uk). This site, while looking at all aspects of school leadership, has a substantial programme of CPD linked to the use of ICT in schools. An important part of its programme involves communication via discussion groups.

- The Office for Standards in Education (www.ofsted.gov.uk). This website includes all inspection reports of schools and LEAs, copies of which can be easily downloaded.

- The Qualifications and Curriculum Authority (www.qca.gov.uk). The QCA is responsible for the National Curriculum and how it is assessed.

- The National Curriculum website (www.nc.uk.net) provides all the content of the National Curriculum and can easily be searched, with downloadable material. Downloads are usually available in two versions. PDF (Portable Document Format) allows the document to be printed out exactly as it would look when in its published form. Your computer needs to have the program Adobe Acrobat installed, but this is a free piece of software that can be downloaded from the Internet. Documents are also usually available in Microsoft Word format, which may lose some of the formatting but does allow the text to be easily incorporated into your own documentation. Do not waste time typing when you can easily download most of the National Curriculum materials you will ever require.

- The Curriculum Online website (www.curriculumonline.gov.uk) lets you find out which products can be purchased with your e-learning credits. This is an education search engine linked specifically to both the National Curriculum and Curriculum Online approved products. It is planned that you will be able to spend your e-learning credits using this website, and they will be truly digital, but a date has not yet been set for this development.

- Teachernet (www.teachernet.gov.uk) is called a portal. It provides links for most of the other relevant sites, so you just need to log on to Teachernet, and you will be able to access most other sites very easily. This is also where you will find free resources that teachers are happy to share with their colleagues.

How should I develop a scheme of work for ICT?

The ICT coordinator should produce a framework identifying the strands of ICT that need to be covered in each term, and should supplement this with the applications that need to be considered for use in each year group, together with a focus on the kinds of skills that they should have developed in that application. Discuss this overall plan at a meeting of year coordinators.

This can now be used during year planning meetings to identify issues such as which pieces of work will be drafted and redrafted using a word processor and which topics will make use of data inputting and interpretation of graphical output. This is also the stage where particular content-rich CD-ROM based products can be selected, and where resource issues, such as the purchase of new pieces of software or hardware, can be discussed.

You will find a scheme of work for ICT available on the DfES Standards Site, but the most effective scheme of work is one that has been developed by a group of committed professionals, taking into account the particular aims of the school and the needs of its particular children. While it is quite correct to say that you should not all have to 'reinvent the wheel', education does require people to develop their own ideas and to innovate, not to stagnate. There is a great deal of support available for the ICT coordinator to develop the school's scheme of work for ICT, much of which is available on-line.

On the Standards Site of the DfES you will find a detailed scheme of work for ICT broken up into units for each year. These units are carefully matched to the National Curriculum programmes of study, so by completing all units you will have covered National Curriculum requirements. These are the units of the Key Stage 1 and 2 Scheme of Work for ICT (QCA/DfES 2000):

Unit 1A	An introduction to modelling.
Unit 1B	Using a word bank.
Unit 1C	The information around us.
Unit 1D	Labelling and classifying.
Unit 1E	Representing information graphically: pictograms.
Unit 1F	Understanding instructions and making things happen.
Unit 2A	Writing stories: communicating information using text.
Unit 2B	Creating pictures.
Unit 2C	Finding information.
Unit 2D	Routes: controlling a floor turtle.
Unit 2E	Questions and answers.
Unit 3A	Combining text and graphics
Unit 3B	Manipulating sound.
Unit 3C	Introduction to databases.
Unit 3D	Exploring simulations.
Unit 3E	E-mail.
Unit 4A	Writing for different audiences.
Unit 4B	Developing images using repeating patterns.
Unit 4C	Branching databases.
Unit 4D	Collecting and presenting information: questionnaires and pie charts.
Unit 4E	Modelling effects on screen.

The Scheme of Work is *not* compulsory, although the National Curriculum is. You can therefore use the Scheme of Work just as it is, or use it as a basis, and amend it to fit in with your school's particular circumstances, or, of course, you need not use it at all. However, as a starting point it provides some excellent resources. Looking at the units you can see that they are broken down into activities, with an introduction called *setting the scene*, some short *focused tasks* and one *integrated task*.

Looking at Unit 4B, Developing images using repeating patterns, for example, you can see that the setting the scene task suggests that children are reminded how cut, paste and copy are used with text, and are told how they can also be used when working with images.

The series of focused tasks then gives children the ICT skills and techniques to manipulate graphic images. They learn how to use stamps, or the copy tool, to alter the size of the brush tool, to select areas, copy and resize them, to use 'save as' to keep drafts of their work and to use a range of effects such as reflection and symmetry.

The integrated task for the unit is then described.

Learning objective

Children should learn to use ICT to use the skills and techniques learnt to organise, reorganise and communicate ideas and to select suitable information and media and prepare it for processing using ICT.

Possible teaching activities

Show the class a mixed media collage, such as *Guitar* by Pablo Picasso, and discuss some of the techniques used. Encourage children to find material that can be scanned, e.g. from newspapers or magazines. Ask children to use the various techniques learnt to incorporate the scanned images in order to create composite images, based on direct observation of musical instruments. Encourage them to focus on particular details, such as tuning pegs or keys. Each child could be given a different viewpoint. Remind them of the importance of saving drafts. Ask children to print out multiple copies of their work and use the printouts, together with other collected images, to make a mixed media collage.

Learning outcomes

Children use a variety of materials, created on and away from the computer, and use them to make a final image.

Here there is a clear introduction, some short focused skill-based activities and a longer integrated task that allows children to practise their newly learned skills in an interesting context.

Your role in producing the school's own scheme of work is now very much a coordinating one, seeing how the children's ICT skills can be developed through their use in interesting activities that link effectively across the curriculum. This issue is looked at further in Chapter 8.

Information and Communication Technology (QCA/DfES 2003) provides a very useful analysis of the sort of computer hardware and software that is essential to cover the Key Stages 1 and 2 National Curriculum for ICT. It suggests the following hardware and software:

Hardware requirements

- Access to networked computers through a mixed model of suites and clusters or standalone machines.
- Access to e-mail and the world wide web.
- Multimedia machines.
- Colour printers.
- A scanner, digital still camera and video camera with associated software.
- A 'floor turtle' or robot.
- A control interface with associated switches, sensors, buzzers, lights and motors.
- An Intel play microscope.
- A means of whole-class teaching using a data projector and/or interactive whiteboard.

Software requirements

- Software that allows children to move and match words and pictures.
- Word banks, a WYSIWYG (what you see is what you get) word processor.
- Paint and object-based drawing software.
- Clip art files on familiar topics.
- An Internet browser to search using key words, indexes and menus.
- A range of CD-ROM titles and web-based resources.
- E-mail.
- An electronic 'Fuzzy Felt' style program or object-based graphics package.
- A simple music composition program or means of recording and editing sounds.

- A simple multimedia authoring program.

- A graphing program capable of drawing pictograms, bar charts, pie charts and line graphs.

- Flat file and branching databases.

- A simple spreadsheet.

- A turtle graphics program that includes the use of repeats and procedures.

- A control program that includes sensing.

- Simulations.

Main teaching and learning issues

- The leadership of the ICT coordinator is of vital importance if a school is to move forward in e-learning.

- The production of an ICT policy should not be just a paper exercise.

- As the ICT resource within a school increases, technical assistance becomes even more vital.

CHAPTER

4

Assessment and Reporting of ICT

What are we really assessing and how should it be done?

A pen, pencil and ruler are used extensively day in and day out by children in all subjects, and computer applications have a similar role. In the same way that much time and effort goes into teaching children how to use pens, pencils and rulers early on in their school career, so children now need to be taught how to use a computer. However, as the children get older they no longer have lessons on how to use a pencil, although comments might well be made about the illegibility of their writing undertaken as part of a history topic. So it is also likely that children will be undertaking tasks in, say, geography during which comments will need to be made about their ICT capability. Your learning objectives for a particular lesson will undoubtedly cover concepts, knowledge and skills related to both geography and ICT. You may or may not decide to share with the children what you hope they are to gain from the activity, but there may come a time when it is useful to make it clear that you are looking for both competent ICT skills and sound geography content.

This becomes particularly important when you give children opportunities for choice. What will you do with the child who never chooses to make use of an ICT application, and only undertakes computer work in focused ICT activities? What do you do with the child who always wants to use the computer and will never, for example, do artwork using paint and paper? This emphasises how important it is for you to be clear about your teaching objectives and the extent to which you will use ICT in achieving them.

It is vital that you ask children key questions that require them to reflect on the appropriateness of their use of ICT, and this may require you to limit their freedom to some extent. This needs to be done sensitively, perhaps by setting a 'rule' that whenever they feel that the computer would be the most appropriate tool for their work, they need to convince you that their argument is sound. This clearly means that teachers also need to know when it is appropriate to use ICT. I remember seeing a child who had carefully produced a drawing for a project in which he was engaged proudly showing a teacher what he had produced. The response of 'That's fine, now copy it on the computer using a paint program' did not seem to be making the best use of the child's time. We must not feel all responses that are not ICT-based are inferior, and no more should we reluctantly admit ICT into the classroom with a Luddite attitude.

Imagine you are teaching children how to use a spreadsheet. You would show them the basic structure, give them some technical terminology such as 'cell' or 'formula', perhaps show them some examples of what they can be used for, then demonstrate how to build a very simple spreadsheet. You could assess their understanding of that particular lesson in two ways, by giving them a test, or by asking them to make their own simple spreadsheet. The test would be relatively easy to administer and mark, and the children designing their own spreadsheet would probably require help and assistance. But which method would be the most appropriate?

As in many cases regarding assessment it is much easier to assess the less important aspects of learning. We must avoid the temptation to concentrate on assessing those things that are easy to assess, and missing out things that are much more important. It is also quite easy to assess things that you can actually see, but much harder to find out what a child has actually learned.

What kind of assessment am I interested in?

There are a number of ways of categorising assessment, but a useful way related to ICT is by using the terms formative, diagnostic and summative.

Formative (assessment for learning)

Formative assessment is the way in which you obtain information about a child's performance, which you then use to guide your subsequent teaching. An important feature of formative assessment is that it can be usefully shared with children so that they are aware of their particular strengths and weaknesses. Sometimes a computer program can provide children with this kind of feedback. Consider a program that gives children a series of problems. When their response is entered into the computer they will be told 'Well done, that answer is correct', or, if it is wrong, they will be told how they might get it right next time. This feedback is formative assessment. It is a particularly positive form of assessment when used in this way, because the program can be (although currently this will not be the case with all such programs) very sophisticated in the amount and nature of the feedback that is given. Sometimes, you as the teacher will undertake the formative assessment. When a child completes a desktop published newsheet, for example, you are likely to give detailed feedback, some of which is likely to be positive, and other elements of which will identify ways in which you think the work could be improved. The term 'assessment for learning' emphasises that this is a vital and integral part of the learning process.

Diagnostic

Diagnostic assessment is the type of information that increasingly you are able to obtain from an integrated learning system, virtual learning environment or CD-ROM. The computer logs responses to children's answers, and the number of attempts that they make on each question. The feedback you might get from this would be that all the multiplication questions are answered very quickly and wrongly, whereas the addition and subtraction questions are being thought about for longer, and the answers are generally correct. This would lead you to think that the child does not know how to do multiplication, or does not understand that it is multiplication that is required in this series of questions. They do not understand, so just give up and go to the next one. You have made your diagnosis and will now talk to the child about his or her understanding of what is required. There are also computer products, such as Assess-it, that enable you to analyse pupil data for diagnostic purposes.

Diagnostic assessment also occurs when you look very carefully at the work that children produce and, usually through a process of analysing children's mistakes, identify their strengths and particularly weaknesses. For example, you see a piece of word-processed work produced by a Year 1 child. It is written well, with few mistakes, but contains no upper case letters. You look at the same child's handwritten work and find that she uses upper case letters at the beginning of all sentences. It would appear that this child does not know, or has forgotten, about the 'shift' key. A demonstration to this child will be necessary the next time she uses the computer.

Summative (assessment of learning)

Summative assessment is in many ways the least useful in terms of children's learning, but often the element that is seen as most important. Level statements and external examination results are the most obvious examples of summative assessment. It is categorised by the fact that a wide range of capabilities, skills and knowledge are 'simplified' into a number, letter or level that is believed to be an assessment of children's learning. This leads us to look at the National Curriculum assessment levels for ICT.

How should I use the National Curriculum Level Statements for ICT?

National Curriculum assessment is not about a checklist of whether a child can cut and paste text between applications, or enter data into a database program, but about far broader statements related to generalised concepts and skills.

It is quite difficult to get to grips with the whole statements but the teacher's guide for the ICT Scheme of Work (QCA/DfES 2003) attempts to identify the significant features that make one level different from the next. The website www.ncaction.org.uk provides exemplification material that relates to each level statement. The activities are summarised below.

Level 1 is characterised by their use of ICT to *explore options* and *make choices* to *communicate meaning*. Children develop *familiarity* with simple ICT tools. For example, children use an art package to create a farmyard scene using 'stamps' of animals. They position the animals on the screen using a mouse and some are shown how to change the size of the animals by using a simple scaling tool. The children understand that they have been able to make choices about what the picture looks like. They then print the pictures and discuss them.

This example illustrates aspects of work at Level 1. The children *demonstrate familiarity* with using the mouse to select, scale and organise images on the screen. They *explore options* using

ICT to *make choices to produce different outcomes.* They *talk about the use of ICT* to create images, comparing it with other methods.

Level 2 is characterised by the *purposeful* use of ICT to achieve *specific outcomes.* For example, children use a music package to explore different sounds and consider the mood of the music. They use a mouse to select and place musical phrases on to a grid, and reorganise the sequence and edit the tempo. They devise words for their composition and perform it as a class. When discussing their work with the teacher, they give reasons for the final choice of musical phrases.

This example illustrates aspects of work at Level 2. The children use ICT *purposefully to investigate options* and *amend* their work. They *use and describe the effects* of aspects of the software that allow them to make changes to the sequence, sound and tempo of their musical composition.

Level 3 is characterised by the use of ICT to *develop ideas* and *solve problems. Lines of enquiry* are followed and the results taken into account in *successive steps.* For example, children are taught to use a control box to make bulbs flash at different speeds. They are asked to make a model of some traffic lights and create a set of instructions to make the lights work properly. Where necessary children make changes to their instructions.

This example illustrates aspects of work at Level 3. Children *develop* their work to create a *sequence of instructions to control devices* to achieve a *specific outcome.*

Level 4 is characterised by the *combination and refining* information from various sources. Children *interpret* and question the *plausibility* of information. For example, children produce a multimedia presentation as part of a project about festivals and celebrations, collecting information from a variety of sources, including books, photographs and interviews. They combine a scanned image, text and sound files to create a page in a multimedia presentation. They use ICT to record spoken explanations and incorporate the sound files on the page to create hyperlinks to explanations, showing they are aware of their audience.

This example illustrates aspects of work at Level 4. The children are able to *combine and refine different forms of information from a variety of sources.* They present information in different forms and, in producing hyperlinked explanations, *show an awareness* of the needs of the intended *audience.*

Level 5 is characterised by *combining the use of ICT tools* within the *overall structure* of an ICT solution. Children critically evaluate the *fitness for purpose* of work as it progresses.

The expectation is that the average Year 2 child will operate at Level 2, a Year 4 child at Level 3 and a Year 6 child at Level 4.

The levels concentrate on a child's ability to use ICT in useful and appropriate ways in the context of meaningful classroom activities. They are 'best fit' descriptions, not tickbox assessments. An important feature of the higher levels is the independence that children need to be able to demonstrate in terms of using a computer program for a task, rather than some other approach, or selecting between a range of programs in order to undertake a particular activity.

Am I assessing ICT or something else?

ICT is a tool and as such it must be used appropriately in all the subjects of the primary curriculum. This does, however, raise problems. For example, when a child completes a piece of work in, say, history that utilises ICT skills, what criteria are you going to use in order to assess it? You can envisage the scenario of a well presented newspaper layout, simulating a newspaper of the seventeenth century, but containing a great deal of inaccurate historical information. What feedback do you give to the child? You obviously designed the activity to cover objectives from both the ICT and the history National Curriculum documents, so you probably need to give feedback on both elements of the task individually.

Is assessing ICT all about skills and techniques, or is there something more?

It is important to realise that there is much more to ICT than gaining confidence and expertise in handling equipment. This would be analogous to saying that we develop skills of using a pen with children solely so that they can make marks on paper. The real development is the higher-order skills that we can develop through using ICT that would be impossible or difficult to develop in any other way.

Essentially we use ICT to develop higher-order thinking skills. We can select and classify information without a computer, but it can be done much more effectively with the sort and graphics capabilities available with databases. You can interpret and analyse data given to you in a book, but it is a far more realistic situation if you do it for real up-to-the-minute data available from the Internet. You can explore mathematical relationships on paper, by undertaking large numbers of calculations, but a more extensive exploration can be undertaken by using a spreadsheet. In order to analyse data you need to be aware of the context in which it was collected and the information that the data can provide you with.

Collecting temperature data manually every five minutes for 24 hours would be impossible logistically, but a computer can be used to do it. Plotting the data onto a graph would be a task far beyond the capability and comprehension of many young children, but by getting the computer to display the graph you are able to get children to discuss what this line going up and down shows us. And very young children are able to start thinking about how to relate a line that goes up and down with temperatures that change and with day and night. Above all, as children develop their capability in ICT, the technical skills become less important and the thinking skills become more important, this being evidenced by the level statements.

How can you make sure that the quality of presentation and the complexity of the technology used does not mask poor quality content and learning?

It is very important that assessment of ICT work is carried out by people with experience of the possibilities of current software packages. Let us take a few examples. Modern word processors can identify incorrectly spelled words as they are being typed. When one is identified, the child needs to click on it and is then given a list of possible alternatives from which to select. This would appear to be an extremely effective way of highlighting incorrect spelling, and providing children with an efficient way of correcting it.

There is, however, another feature in some packages called AutoCorrect. This consists of a customised list of words, which is intended to focus on common mistyping of words. You would type 'acommodate' into the first column of the AutoCorrect database, and 'accommodate' into the second column. Every time you typed in the word 'acommodate' it would immediately be changed into the correct spelling. If you are responsible for putting in the data to the feature then you would be responsible in some way for the learning, but if you are not, it is very easy for the computer to correct your mistakes without the child realising that she has made any. While spell checking is a way of a child interacting with the computer program, and hence being in a position to identify problem spellings and perhaps learn as a result of this, the AutoCorrect feature does not involve interaction, and may indeed encourage children to be less accurate in their text input, because the computer will automatically change it for them.

In terms of assessing a child's performance, the AutoCorrect feature requires no skill on behalf of the child, and their actual knowledge of spelling could be worse than that of another child in the class, but the product generated by the computer would be word perfect. Could this child be seen to be cheating, or is she, very intelligently, making full use of the power that computer programs are able to deliver?

Let us take a further example. Many computer programs now have 'wizards' (which would previously have been called macros – not nearly as exciting a word), which guide the user step-by-step through relatively complicated processes. Designing a newsletter using a desktop publishing package would be a typical example. It is an extremely complicated task to design a newsletter from scratch but, using a wizard, the layout can be created extremely quickly, and it also tells you where to type in your text, and where to import your graphic elements, clip art and photographs. A child who uses a wizard follows clear instructions and is constrained by the design that the program allows. A child who does not use a wizard will be using a considerably wider range of technical and design skills, but it is possible that the finished product will not be of as high a quality. If the teacher is unaware of the two vastly different processes that the children went through, is she likely to assess the two children's work in a meaningful way?

In both of these examples, it is important to reflect that you would be wishing to assess the content of the work that the children were presenting, as well as its presentation.

The ICT is there, but what about real learning?

I am sure everyone can relate to the following scenario. Children are asked to do a project on Queen Elizabeth I. You get three groups of responses. One group consists of pages and pages of information about Elizabeth I copied out from a range of reference books. The same information is repeated several times, as it occurred in several articles. There are some well drawn pictures copied out of a number of the books. The second group of work consists of two pages of clearly typed text about the queen, and a printout of a painting of her when she first came to the throne. The third group, made up of both handwritten and computer-generated text, focuses in on particular aspects of Queen Elizabeth's life. It clearly makes use of information from different sources, but it is also clear that the children have interacted with the information and produced something of their own. In what ways should our assessment of these three types of outcome be undertaken?

The first group have not made any use of ICT at all. Perhaps they have not got access to it at home, or perhaps they are not interested in it. They took a great deal of time over their project, and most enjoyed copying the drawings. When asked about things they had written, some clearly did not understand some of the longer words and more sophisticated forms of expression that they have copied out of encyclopaedias with a very high reading age.

The second group have made some use of ICT, but it is clearly at a fairly basic level. They have undertaken a search on 'Queen Elizabeth I' and have found one article. This they have printed out. They then selected the photograph and printed this out. The pages are stapled together and handed in. One or two of this group have imported the text into a desktop publishing package, added a title and their name, removed the copyright statement and imported the photograph into the centre of the text. On questioning, they appear to know very little about Queen Elizabeth I; in fact it would appear that some children have not even read the article at all.

In the third group some have obviously shown ability with ICT, but others have not. They have, however, all shown an ability to search for particular information and to put it together in a form with which they were happy, and which they could clearly understand. When questioned, it was children in this group who had a clear idea of some aspects of the life of Queen Elizabeth I.

We need to make children aware of the differences between these three outcomes, in particular making it clear to them that presentation is not the only thing that is important.

How can you determine the achievement of individuals when the 'product' is the result of a collaborative effort?

Much of the work that children undertake on a computer is collaborative. In many cases this seems to enhance the learning experience, as children discuss and talk about the issues involved. There will be many times when an activity of this type is not overtly assessed, but what strategies can be used when you do wish to assess children's individual response within a group activity? Clear teacher observation can achieve much, as can asking the group themselves to identify the contributions they have made to the group activity, backed up by teacher records, which will confirm or disagree with the children's views. These differences, used sympathetically, could be the basis for useful discussions about ways of developing and improving group work. Appropriate teacher intervention is also very important. This should be not negative intervention ('Stop doing that') or critical intervention ('That's not very good – do it another way') but supportive and formative intervention ('That's a good start. Can you see any disadvantages of doing it that way? Have you thought about using this approach, which may solve some of your problems?'). The responses from individuals to these interventions will give you a good feel for their individual understanding, and remember that assessment should not be a one-off snapshot, but should be one small piece of evidence that gradually builds up to give you an overall view of the abilities of the child.

To be effective you will probably need to create groups yourself, rather than letting the children always work in friendship groups. There might be times, for example, when you would like some peer tutoring to take place. This should not be viewed as a waste of time for the child who is doing the tutoring, as it is a good way to consolidate understanding by trying to transmit knowledge to other people. It also needs to be identified as a high-profile role, with some limited training given to the children so that they understand that they should not be doing the task for the other child, but assisting and offering useful advice in order to enhance the other child's ICT capability. At other times you may want children of equivalent ability working together on ICT projects, so that they can spark ideas off each other and all move forward together, with appropriate intervention from the teacher.

A class's first exploration of devising a multimedia package could consist of a page of information about each child, which would be put on by each child themselves. After an initial class discussion about the information the class would like to include about themselves, a small team could devise the template for each page. Another team could subsequently build up the front page, which might consist of small thumbnail pictures of each child in the class, which when clicked upon would take you to their particular page.

What techniques can I use to assess children's attainment?

Assessment by observation and questioning

The most important element of assessment is the day-to-day knowledge that the class teacher picks up about the child's abilities and progress in all subjects. All other methods are supplementary to this, providing *aides-mémoire* or evidence of your assessment. We clearly needed to move away from the time when teachers had 'gut feelings' about the abilities of children but failed to keep adequate records about their progress, but the first stages of the National Curriculum overload came about because teachers felt that their own professional judgements were no longer of any worth, and that everything had to be recorded, filed away and photographed to produce a bank of totally independent evidence. If it moved, you assessed it!

Now, thankfully, the professionalism and experience of the teacher should be at the forefront of the teaching and learning (and consequently assessment) programmes, and appropriate evidence is collected to supplement these findings.

There may be times when an adult helper can assist children with particular activities. Provided they are encouraged to assist when required, rather than take over at the first sign of a difficulty, this can greatly enhance children's capability. Note that they are not just assessing, but are helping in the teaching and learning process. A child is typing in her name into a word processor. She has been asked to produce a label for her sandwich box. The helper asks about the size of the font. The child competently changes the font size – it needs to be big so that it can easily be seen, she says. What else could we put on the label? 'A picture would be nice,' says the child and clicks on the clip art symbol of the program. The child is then encouraged to choose a suitable picture, and is reminded how to put the picture in the right place on the screen. The adult here is helping in the scaffolding process as promulgated by Vytgotsky (see Chapter 2), seeing where a child has difficulties and then offering just sufficient support to set her off again, to explore new learning. This adult helper would easily be able to express to the class teacher either verbally or on the appropriate records the progress that the child was making in ICT.

Self-assessment by children themselves

Increasingly, the benefits of children having some responsibility over their own learning are seen to be important, not only because *some* of the administrative elements of the task are transferred from the teacher to the pupil, but also because if children know what is expected of them, they are in a better position to plan and organise their way to get there. It is also more motivating for many children if they know what the final outcome of the activity is likely to be. By having an achievable target many especially motivated children will make great strides themselves.

Consider how you would react if you went on an ICT training course. You are not told what program you will be using, and you are not told what you will be expected to achieve by the end of the day. You are given instructions in small chunks, initially being shown how to open up particular computer files, then how to use particular tools in a desktop publishing package. You go through a series of small tasks practising the use of a number of techniques and then finally you are set an activity to design a poster for a car boot sale.

I do not think you would be likely to return to that particular in-service provider, even though the standard of the actual training might have been very high. You would have had little motivation, because you did not know what you were supposed to be doing, the activity itself was irrelevant to your professional work and no account was taken of what your own personal capability in ICT was.

Some children, particularly with computers at home, could be put into a very similar position. If you provide children with more freedom to use computers in appropriate ways and make them responsible for recording this progress, then many of them are likely to be more motivated. If you provide children with some indication of the range of ICT skills that they will need to show they have developed over a period of time, this will enable them all to know the direction in which they should be heading, and it also provides an approach for all abilities. Those children who are less confident can approach it as a step-by-step process: 'This time I do some word-processing I will use some different fonts and use "centred" and "left aligned" text. Next time I will include a clip art picture in my document.' But children who are capable ICT users could, justifiably, miss out huge chunks of the earlier stages and always produce well designed documents including clip art, graphic elements, charts and graphs, because they know what will eventually be expected of them. This gives rise to real progression, with children striving to make the most of the power of the computer they have in front of them, and, because of the nature of many programs, it is very easy to organise. You do not need to set up different software, as the children themselves will just be able to use the more advanced tools when they become aware of them, and they are unlikely to run out of features. The general user of a word-processing program makes use of approximately 30 per cent of the available functionality.

There are clearly challenges with such an approach. You need to prevent children from jumping ahead to more complex activities when they are unable to use and understand the more basic features. This will lead to demotivation on both the child's and the teacher's part, with the child continually getting stuck and asking for help, and the teacher getting frustrated by spending so much time with one child undertaking an activity that is too difficult for him or her and in the end doing the task for the child. I must confess that I have had this feeling of frustration when dealing with students who dismiss the carefully structured programme of help sheets 'because they understand it all' and then monopolise your attention when failing to complete 'something they have always wanted to do' because they clearly do not understand the basics. There is always a balance to be made between freedom and structure, and clearly, as always, it is the intervention of the teacher in the process that is important in order to assist the child in understanding where that balance actually is.

This approach also relies on the fact that the teacher is either competent in the use of the program to a high level or confident enough to admit that he or she does not know how every feature of every program works, and that very few people actually do. What is important at that level is that the children are aware of suitable strategies for solving such problems by using, for example, on-line help files or paper-based manuals. Certainly, a regular feature of any primary classroom could be children telling their classmates how to do new things with particular computer programs. A session like this pointing out two or three little techniques that have been discovered is an excellent way of developing everyone's capability, both children and teachers. (Did you know that Shift F3 in Microsoft Word 6 cycles the highlighted text through all lower case, all upper case and lower case with upper case first letter, which is very useful when you have mistakenly left caps lock on?)

What should self-assessment records look like?

Generally the assessment sheets should look professionally produced and be tabular in structure. They should be written at a certain language level, using terminology that is appropriate for the children involved. There should be spaces for the children to indicate that they have undertaken the particular work, and space to identify the activity that was involved. There should also be space for the teacher to write comments and to confirm that the child has satisfactorily completed the task.

Self-assessment sheets take many forms, and it is possible for Key Stage 1 and 2 children to be offered accreditation in order to provide them with physical evidence of the level of their ICT capability.

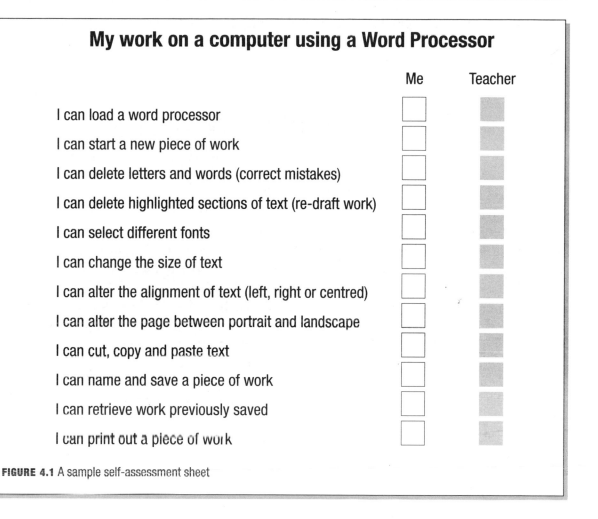

FIGURE 4.1 A sample self-assessment sheet

You might also decide that you want to collect children's ICT work to form a portfolio. Beware of the disadvantages of such an approach. As most of your ICT work will be undertaken in the context of other subjects, it might be more appropriate for it to be included in each subject's folder or exercise book. What would be far more useful would be a school portfolio showing children's work that the school believes shows the standards that need to be achieved to attain the various levels. This should be compiled by the coordinator for ICT, and should be ever changing. It needs to include only three or four pieces of work corresponding to each level statement and provides an extremely useful reference for new members of staff and trainee teachers to gauge the nature and quality of the ICT work that the school expects of children. It is also a useful resource that can be shown to parents, governors and visitors from Ofsted.

We have already discussed the problem of assessing subject content and ICT capability within a single piece of work. One approach to this would be to ask the children to annotate a photocopy of a substantial piece of work undertaken with ICT to highlight the features of the program they used, and why they did so. You would then mark their original work for its subject content, and discuss the annotated photocopy for the ICT element. This would not be a regular occurrence, but it would be useful evidence that could inform your decision as to the level at which the children are operating.

How can I keep effective records of progress in ICT?

There is a need within any school to maintain a record of the activities that a particular class teacher has provided. This needs to be supplemented by more particular details of the activities that individual children have actually engaged in.

The records first need to show overall coverage of ICT use and the progression that is initially planned for. It is likely, for example, that you will introduce children to the ways in which data can be expressed in a graphical form, and the ways in which it can be interpreted. The records would show that all children were given an opportunity both to produce the graphs and to make attempts at interpreting them.

These records are important for class teachers, so that they have a quick way of remembering which of the group have actually undertaken a particular activity. With limited ICT resources, it is inevitable that many of the activities will be spread over fairly long periods of time, so an *aide-mémoire* is essential for the busy classroom teacher. It is also important that there is adequate information to give to trainee teachers on their placements or replacement teachers who might teach the class during periods of illness. It also provides a useful evaluation tool for planning future work. If, for example, everyone in the group found the activity extremely straightforward, it might suggest that in future years a further of degree of complexity could be added to the task, or that the particular piece of software used this year was far easier to handle than that which had been used in previous years.

As with any recording system, there has to be an appropriate balance between the time taken to fill in the information and the detail of information recorded. An extremely quick system may hold so little information as to be useless, whereas a more sophisticated recording system may be theoretically extremely useful, but there is insufficient time in the day to record it effectively, so what you get is an incomplete record, which again is useless.

In the not too distant future it will be very easy to keep these records in a computer-based format. Again children could put in their own data, which would then be confirmed by the teacher. The teacher's part of the recording system would be password protected, so children would not be able to enter their own confirmation, and children would only have access to their own records, so they could not alter their classmates' results.

Remember that in this system we are looking at fairly basic information. Many recording systems exist, but a common one uses a triangle, with / indicating that the child needs more help, $\wedge$ indicating partial understanding and a complete triangle indicating full understanding, marked against a number of checking points.

Checking Points	
1	
2	
3	
4	
5	
6	
7	
8	
9	

Name	Checking Points								
	1	2	3	4	5	6	7	8	9

/ needs more help   ∧ partial understanding   △ full understanding

FIGURE 4.2 An example of a class recording sheet

What sort of report should I be able to provide for parents?

Increasingly the role of reporting is taking on much more focus, particularly when much of the output to parents can now easily be computer generated. (See Chapter 6 for a discussion of using ICT to produce reports.)

A good report first needs to comment on what the child can do, and this obviously needs to be set in the context of the experiences that the child has had over a period of time. The report should also comment upon special accomplishments and the difficulties that have been encountered.

There should be comments about the child's level of attainment, and this needs to be set in some form of context. It is probably more useful to discuss children's level in relation to children of their age throughout the country than to discuss their position within their own class. For this sort of comparison to be meaningful, there needs to be background information about the overall ability of the individual class itself.

It is useful to identify the way forward, in terms of future topics and activities as well as more specific advice on ways in which the child could be assisted to improve. As always, care must be taken to ensure that no undue pressure is put upon parents to, for example, spend money on software, or even a computer, in order to help a child to develop his or her expertise, although clearly such advice to children or parents who already have appropriate equipment would be more useful. The school clearly needs to have a strategy to deal with children who do not have home or community access to a computer, perhaps by setting up lunchtime or after-school homework or computer clubs.

How can I find the time to do all this planning, assessing and recording?

It is wrong to perceive assessment, recording and reporting, and even teaching and learning, as clearly delineated activities. They are all integrated parts of what goes on in the classroom. Assessment in all its forms should be a natural part of teaching and learning activities. It should arise from current classroom practice and it should build upon children's previous experience. Let us look at a very much simplified classroom situation, to see how all the elements interweave.

As part of a book project each child is asked to produce an illustration relating to a different part of a story. They are encouraged to select clip art pictures from a reference book and then to import their selected image into a paint program, where they edit it at pixel level so that it matches their requirements. They also use the paint program to add additional features to the picture, including speech bubbles with text. All the children have used the paint package before and the records show that they all achieved at least partial understanding in all the previous checking points, except for two children who were absent on the last occasion.

The ICT checking points for this activity are:

Is the child able to:

- select an appropriate clip art image;
- import the image into the paint program;
- use the magnifying tool and change colours and shape at pixel level;
- include appropriate text in speech bubbles?

The activity is done in pairs, and as there are only two computers available, all the other children are working on other literacy tasks related to making their books.

Of the two children who were away, you know one has a computer at home and works well with her friend, who was present at the last session. You decide that they will work as one pair. You decide that the second pair should include the other previously absent child and a very capable ICT child who is competent at peer tutoring.

You talk to the whole class about the activity, reminding them of their previous work with the paint program, and then showing them on the interactive whiteboard some of the clip art pictures that are available on the computer. You talk about the importance of choosing appropriate images for their story, and you briefly show the whole class how to use the magnifying tool in order to personalise small elements of the picture.

Although the children are working in pairs, you want each child to produce their own picture for their part of the story. Your clear instructions are that while each of the pair should assist and support the other, the child whose picture they are actually working on will have control over the mouse and keyboard, and will be responsible for the final decisions. In this way, you have the benefits of sharing of ideas and skills, but you do not have the problem of one person taking over the whole activity. You have previously asked the group to think about what they wanted in their illustration, and to sketch out their ideas.

You set the children working at the computer and ask them to select the clip art they want from the reference manual. You talk to the rest of the class and get them started on a literacy group activity. You return to the computers and ask for a volunteer to go through the process of importing the clip art and magnifying the image. The child who was absent, but who has a computer at home, volunteers, and carefully goes through the whole process with a few minor mistakes, which she immediately rectifies. You provide additional explanation as she goes through the processes. You are now clear that this child can be recorded as 'fully understanding' the previous art package activity. You now leave the group for ten minutes, saying that any problems that develop during that time should be attempted to be solved within the group. By doing this you are not letting them flounder for an excessive period of time if they are really stuck, but you are giving them freedom to try to solve their own problems, a vital part of learning, without seeking the much easier route of asking you what to do next.

You now return to each pair and discuss what they have been doing. You comment positively initially, but then identify some ways in which the work could be made better. 'The colours you have chosen are really bright and stand out very well from the background. One of the people in the picture is very much smaller than the other and as they are supposed to be sisters of similar age, this needs to be changed. You seem to have removed too much of that person's leg as you have been editing the image. You need to change back some of the pixels to their original colour.' Here is your formative assessment, feeding back to the children in a positive way the issues they need to consider in order to improve the finished product. After a further twenty minutes ask the children to save their images and to assist the other child in the pair to develop their own picture. Again, after ten minutes, provide the group with some formative feedback as to the progress that is being made.

Just before the end of the session look at the work produced by all four children. With a brief discussion and the pictures in front of you, it will clear which of the checking points have been achieved, and these can be marked off there and then. You will also have enhanced your knowledge about the four individuals and the level of their ICT competence. You will have noticed, for example, that two of the children were very confident in their manipulation of the picture, and quickly achieved some very high-quality products. The other two children were a little slower in manipulating the picture and had more difficulty in importing the clip art pictures, but they were supported very well by their two classmates, and you feel that they will be able to finish the product effectively by themselves later on in the week.

You have also been able to make some initial impressions of the level at which these children are operating in terms of handling information. At this stage you feel the first two, more ICT capable, children are approaching Level 4, where a main emphasis is on combining and refining information. The other two children seem to be operating at a competent Level 3 as they followed a particular line of enquiry.

Is there software to help with assessing children?

There is much software that helps teachers to create plans, match learning objectives and record children's marks or levels. This type of software really just records assessment data. There are, however, a few packages, such as AssessIT, that do more than record, actually providing teachers with detailed information about individual children's progress.

By taking Key Stage test results as a baseline the software can indicate target levels for each year for individual children. The software includes tables of national statistics and so is able to make comparisons between progress in your school and progress in similar schools in other parts of the country. It is also interactive, in that targets will be reset if children exceed some of their interim targets. Most positively, it provides real data that teachers can use to analyse a child's or group of children's progress. AssessIT also instantly highlights children who are falling below their projected paths and produces an intervention strategy document, which provides prompts to teachers to get the children back on target.

In effect, this software works independently to do what the management section of an integrated learning system does. The lesson that should be learned is that teachers need to be aware of how to analyse the information they have and how to make best use of it. Research has shown that this is often a weakness in the effective use of integrated learning system packages.

Main teaching and learning issues

- Assessment is part of the normal teaching and learning situation.

- Evidence gradually builds up over time, not through specific assessment activities.

- If you do not give children the opportunity to work more autonomously, then they will never be able to demonstrate an ability to work at Level 4 or above.

Children in Control of the Computer

What are the content-free ICT packages that children should be able to use?

One of the advantages of computer software is that it is extremely flexible. It can be used by children in an endless number of ways. While this creativity is a powerful motivating factor, it can also cause problems if children cannot find out how to do things properly. As a teacher, therefore, it is important that you have a clear idea of the ways in which the skills and techniques are developed. It is here that the power of a graphical interface with its common menu structure means that many of the skills developed by children when using one program will be truly transferable to other ones.

This chapter looks at the wide range of computer programs that can be used by primary age children and that will enhance their ICT capability. They are generally content-independent programs. You and the children choose what to put into them. Subsequent chapters draw upon this background, showing how the basic ICT knowledge, skills and techniques can be used in different curriculum areas. We will also look at the main teaching and learning outcomes that can be achieved with each type of program. This is not the point at which to discuss individual named programs. This will be done during discussions of the practical uses to which these programs can be put in the primary classroom in Chapters 7 to 10. The computer is being used here as an extremely creative and open-ended tool, over which the child could have complete control. The teacher's task is to ensure that they are able to develop their skills in a clearly structured way through motivating and worthwhile activities.

Word processing

This is probably the most common type of computer program in use in all walks of life today. At its simplest it allows text to be entered via a keyboard and this appears on a screen, which simulates a sheet of paper. A good way of evaluating the usefulness of a particular program is to consider how similar activities are traditionally undertaken and how, by using a computer, the learning associated with the activity could be enhanced. Writing in schools has relied extensively on paper, pencils and pens for some considerable time and before that there was chalk and a slate. These media have the advantage of being relatively cheap, readily accessible and portable. Why should we consider replacing them with an expensive computer?

The most powerful argument is undoubtedly that of being able to edit the material quickly and effectively. If I were to be writing this chapter traditionally I would expect to have sheets of paper with headings, some with ideas and possible diagrams and others with some attempts at coherent writing, but with inevitable crossings out, arrows and a multitude of abbreviations and annotations. This material would then, at the very least, have to be rewritten, reviewed and edited, and then a final version would be produced. Instead, I have a computer screen, with the headings I intend to write about providing me with an outline of the document. I type text in the appropriate places as the ideas develop. This can encourage more engagement with the text because the editing process is far easier and more interactive. It takes a great more willpower to motivate oneself to make significant changes to a third draft that has been handwritten or typed than it does to make a few improvements to the sixth or seventh draft of a document that is stored in an electronic format.

So a word-processing program can be actively used to encourage children to draft and redraft their written work and hence encourage them to interact more effectively with text. Another important feature of a word processor is the spell check facility. With careful structuring this can greatly assist in developing children's spelling. They could, for example, be encouraged to make up their own spelling word bank of the words that the spell check program identifies they have spelt incorrectly. They can also be encouraged to use the thesaurus to extend their vocabulary.

Other features of word-processing programs can be used to enhance the presentation of the finished product. Different sizes of text, different fonts and different spacings and alignments can all be used to good effect. Increasingly word processors are also able to speak the words as they are being typed in and this can be a very motivating feature that emphasises the link between the word as a sound and the word as a pattern of letters.

We have looked so far at putting in information using the computer keyboard, but other options are available. Children will find that using a mouse – a device for moving a pointer around the screen and for selecting particular options – can save time. This is a vital area of ICT skill development and needs to be introduced to children at a very early age. Overlay keyboards can be used to provide a mechanism for inputting whole words at a time into word-processing packages and increasingly very young children are making use of interactive whiteboards to input text in group or whole-class teaching situations.

There is software that allows you to speak into a microphone and the words you speak appear in your word processor. Currently, these systems rarely work in a school situation as effectively as might have been hoped because each child has to go through a procedure to teach the computer the way he or she speaks, and it also requires very little background noise – hardly the typical conditions for a primary school classroom.

Main teaching and learning issues

- Encourage children to develop their mouse skills.

- Use the word processor to engage children in manipulating text.

- Drafting and redrafting.

- Teach children how to use the spell check and thesaurus facilities.

- Linking the spoken and written word, with the computer giving one-to-one feedback.

Avoid

- Concentrating on the look of the document at the expense of its content.

- Using too many different fonts in one piece of work.

- Using the word processor solely to copy out a piece of children's work for display.

Spreadsheets

At its simplest a spreadsheet is a method of doing lots of calculations automatically and very quickly. The basic form of the spreadsheet is a series of cells. Each cell can contain some text, a number or a formula. The point of the program is to manipulate numbers very quickly. For example, located in cell C1 is the equation =(A1*B1). This means 'Take the number in cell A1, multiply it by the number in cell B1 and put the result in cell C1'. As soon as you change the number in one of the cells, all the cells that are linked to it are altered as well. In the trivial example in Figure 5.1 this is no great advantage, but where more calculations are involved advantages can be accrued. This links to the other great use of spreadsheets, where 'What if?' investigations can easily be carried out.

	A	B	C	D	E
1	7	12.5	=(A1*B1)	Text	
2					
3					
4					

FIGURE 5.1 A simple spreadsheet

Children in Control of the Computer

Food	Quantity	Cost	Total	
Pizza slices	10	£0.50	£5.00	
Crisps	12	£0.25	£3.00	
Cola (glass)	10	£0.20	£2.00	
Total Cost			£10.00	

FIGURE 5.2 A sample spreadsheet – total cost £10.00

For example, suppose the class has a £10.00 budget for an end-of-term party. What sort of food should they buy, and in what quantities? By using this sort of spreadsheet they can quickly calculate how much more pizza they could buy if they bought cheaper crisps. Again, in this simplistic example, the power of a spreadsheet is not really necessary, but if the list of food got longer and the alternative prices were more extensive, a spreadsheet like this would provide a useful financial model.

Food	Quantity	Cost	Total	
Pizza slices	12	£0.50	£6.00	
Crisps	10	£0.20	£2.00	
Cola (glass)	10	£0.20	£2.00	
Total Cost			£10.00	

FIGURE 5.3 What if we buy cheaper crisps?

Most spreadsheets can be formatted very extensively, with different fonts and text sizes, colours, borders and shading. The design skills needed to produce clear spreadsheets are the same as those that need to be developed in areas such as desktop publishing. It is therefore important when devising activities to make sure that they focus upon the features that are unique to this type of program. In other words, if you want the children to develop the skills pertinent to spreadsheets do not concentrate on formatting their work – these are desktop publishing skills.

Many programs designed as spreadsheets can also be used very effectively as databases. This flexibility is obviously useful, but teachers and children need to be aware of the distinct differences between the two types of activity.

Main teaching and learning issues

- Using formulae is the very essence of spreadsheet work.

- Initially set up spreadsheets to which children can add data.

- Set up spreadsheets to answer 'What if?' questions.

Avoid

- Confusing spreadsheet and database activities.

Databases

A database is no more than a store of information designed to give a clear structure to that information. Fundamentally, it is a huge table with fields along the top and records down the side. Field names identify the categories of information, while records are the collection of fields related to a particular item.

	Fieldname 1	Fieldname 2	Fieldname 3	Fieldname 4
Record 1				
Record 2				
Record 3				

FIGURE 5.4 The basic structure of a database

In the example in Figure 5.5, 'Surname' and 'First Name' are *fields* (columns), while a *record* is all the information pertaining to one person (rows).What different database programs provide is different ways of searching through this basic information to come up with the data that is required. They also provide ways of displaying this information in graphical formats and it is this power that children are likely to use when they first encounter this type of program. At its simplest, which of Figures 5.6 and 5.7 best illustrates the proportion of boys and girls in a particular class?

In the early years of primary school, children should be able to add data to a prepared database and to display this information in meaningful ways. Later on they should be able to design their own database structure to investigate a particular topic in which they have an interest and to interrogate the database to identify new patterns of information.

	Surname	First Name	Age	Hair Colour
1	Andrews	Paulette	8	Blonde
2	Evans	David	8	Black
3	Wilkes	Desdomona	7	Red

FIGURE 5.5 An example of a simple database

Boys	23
Girls	7

FIGURE 5.6 A table showing the number of boys and girls in a class

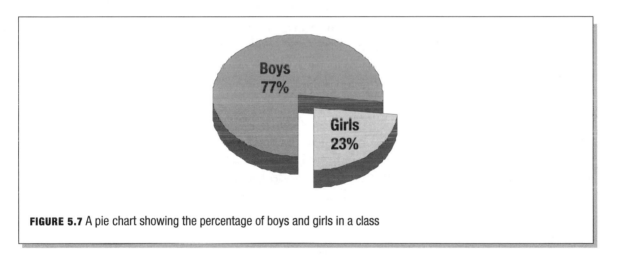

FIGURE 5.7 A pie chart showing the percentage of boys and girls in a class

The question that must be answered is: in what ways is a database more effective than the same information stored on a piece of paper? First, there is the ease with which data can be readily transformed into a helpful graphical representation. At a relatively early age children can learn to analyse the meanings of pie and bar charts long before they have the mathematical or drawing skills to produce them themselves.

Second is the way in which the information can be easily reorganised so that patterns can become more readily identifiable. Sorting a database of the children in a class first by age and then by height, to see if there is a correlation between the two, is a few seconds' work using a computer but a much longer and boring task using pencil and paper. Here the computer can eliminate time-consuming activities to allow you to concentrate on higher-order learning, asking children to investigate and analyse rather than reorganise and copy.

Third is the way in which the computer can search for information very quickly, although it is only when children are using very large databases that this advantage becomes obvious. Looking through a paper database of the class to find out who has got red hair is probably more appropriate than using the searching power of a computer. However, doing the same for the whole school might emphasise the advantage of a computer-based approach.

A point to bring out here is that all information-based CD-ROMs and the entire Internet are databases. They have very sophisticated and well designed graphical interfaces between you and the information, but all they do is search through a carefully organised structure to display on the screen the information that you need. Both CD-ROMs and the Internet are discussed in more detail in later chapters.

The new technical skills that children need to be taught in the area of databases are those associated with interrogating the data. These should be introduced very early on in primary schools when children are using much smaller databases so that they will be able to use the much larger ones effectively.

Typing a word into the *search engine* (a program designed to search for articles containing certain words or groups of words) of a CD-ROM encyclopaedia, for example, is likely to give many articles that contain information on that topic. But is a child going to look through all thirty articles to select the most appropriate information, or is she more likely to look through the first few and disregard the later ones – and, to be honest, what would you be likely to do? So, in order to ensure that we limit the information we are given and that this is the most relevant to our needs, we need to think carefully about how we encourage children to search for information.

A child wanting to find out about London Bridge in a current major CD-ROM encyclopaedia will find no such entry, and so might reasonably expect to search more generally and type in 'Bridges'. This will give information on Robert Seymour Bridges, but nothing about metal and stone structures! If he perseveres and types in 'Bridge', and if he avoids the information about the card game, he will find some useful text and pictures about bridges as structures. He will then be directed to other articles, including 'Tower Bridge, London'. Unfortunately, he will find nothing about London Bridge.

This simple scenario highlights the need for search strategies to be taught to children from very early in their school life. This becomes increasingly important as children are able to use the Internet on a daily basis. As this is nothing more than a worldwide database, single search words are likely to give 100,000 possible articles to explore. This emphasises the need for careful thought about what information we are trying to find out before we even switch on the computer. The time spent in preparatory work done before the search starts could save hours, days or even years in sifting through the articles that the search engine selects.

The strategies required include the framing of useful questions, realising that they have to be phrased in particular ways and probably need to make use of logical operators such as AND, OR and NOT. Although most packages have their own particular way of using these terms (for example, in some databases + in front of a word means it must be included), they all use the principles outlined in these simple examples. If you wanted to find out about Tudor Kings a useful starting point would be articles that contained 'Tudor' AND 'King'. If you were looking for information about holiday resorts in the Mediterranean you might search for 'Resort' AND 'Spain' OR 'Italy' OR 'France'. If you were looking for information about people who use bows and arrows you might use the search 'Archer' NOT 'Geoffrey' OR 'Jeffrey'.

Children also need to be aware of how up-to-date the information is, and also how reliable information from some websites is likely to be. They should be taught suitable research strategies, such as getting information from a number of different sources and comparing it, and always taking note of the date when a website was last updated, or when a CD-ROM was produced.

Main teaching and learning issues

■ Analysis of graphical representations of data can now be done by much younger children than was previously possible.

■ Children should start by adding data to existing databases.

■ Techniques for searching databases are vital new ICT skills that must be taught and practised.

■ Children should be aware of the advantages of computer databases over paper ones.

Avoid

■ Using ICT-based data sources to the exclusion of paper-based ones.

■ Providing young children with too much information from which to select.

■ Unstructured projects that involve searching CD-ROMs and the Internet.

Graphic packages and clip art

While there are many drawing and paint packages available, they basically come as one of two main types.

Consider that a computer screen is made up of a grid of very small rectangles, called pixels. On a typical Windows computer the grid is 1024 by 768, giving a total of 786,432 individual points. In a paint package you have a large number of features that allow you to alter the colour of each of these pixels. You can really think of it as electronic 'painting by numbers'. These are called bitmapped images and because information about the colour of every pixel on the screen needs to be stored they tend to be made up of very large files. Photographs that are scanned into a computer are stored as bitmap files and software is available that can change the colour of

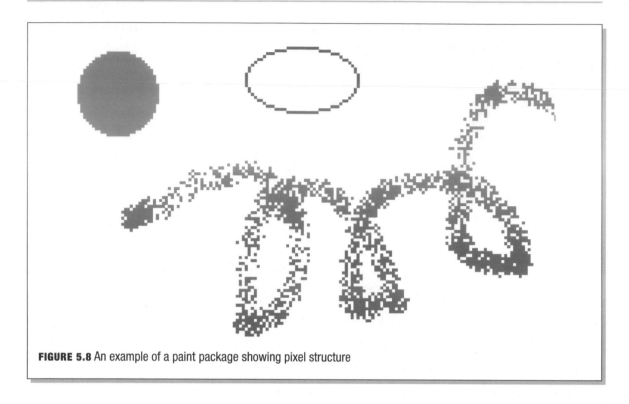

FIGURE 5.8 An example of a paint package showing pixel structure

every pixel. This means that photographs can be retouched by zooming into the photograph and making suitable changes – removing facial blemishes, changing the colour of eyes, removing a person from a photograph altogether. Any picture that is drawn in this way can therefore be edited by changing the colour of individual pixels. One of the major disadvantages of this type of picture is that as you try to enlarge it the 'pixel type' nature of the image becomes more obvious, with lines being seen not as smooth curves but as irregular lines.

A drawing package stores the graphics images in an alternative form – as a series of mathematical equations. If you draw a square in a draw package the information that is stored consists of the size of the square, the position it occupies on the screen and its colour. If you draw a much larger square, the amount of information that has to be stored about the shape is very similar, i.e. size, position and colour. This means that the amount of storage space for drawing files is much less than that required for paint files.

Draw packages also allow images to overlap on different layers, and each component of the drawing can be selected and edited separately, giving considerable control over the finished product. It also means that when the image is enlarged, the values in the mathematical equation are increased proportionally and a clear image is still obtained – not one made up of jagged lines. You should also be aware that some of the more sophisticated graphics packages are able to work with both 'draw' and 'paint' objects.

Other hardware items that you will need to consider when undertaking work with graphics are digital cameras, scanners, drawing pads and good quality colour printers. Digital cameras store the coloured images electronically rather than on film. A scanner converts the

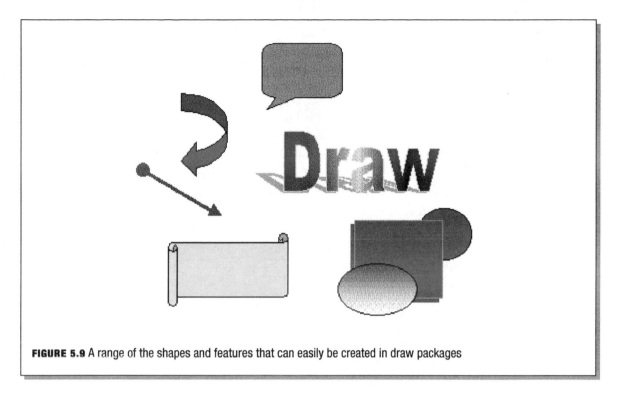

FIGURE 5.9 A range of the shapes and features that can easily be created in draw packages

physical image on a sheet of paper into an electronic image, with each pixel being designated a different colour. Once they are converted into a digital form, they can be manipulated by computer packages, or just printed out using a printer.

Digitising tablets or computer drawing pads consist of a pressure-sensitive drawing board that is connected to a computer and can be used with a range of art packages. A pen-like stylus is used to draw on the board, and the movements are replicated on the screen – there is no mark made on the board itself. The stylus can also operate like a mouse in selecting functions of the software. An interactive whiteboard has similar functions.

The most common types of colour printers are ink-jet and laser printers. Ink-jets are currently the cheapest to buy and they can produce very high-quality images, particularly when printing using glossy photographic paper. However, the cost of consumables (i.e. replacement ink cartridges and photographic paper) is very high and often the running costs outweigh the capital cost of the printer within a few months. Colour ink-jet printers use either four individual colour cartridges – black, cyan, yellow and magenta – or a single colour cartridge which contains reservoirs of cyan, yellow and magenta ink. Although usually more expensive, the versions with the four cartridges generally give a better overall quality, because the black images are created from black ink, rather than a mixture of cyan, yellow and magenta, which can give a more brown colour. Moreover, the separate cartridges only need to be replaced when they are each completely empty, whereas the combined cartridge has to be replaced as soon as the first of the colours runs out, or you get some very funny coloured images. Colour laser printers can now be purchased for about the cost of a typical black and white laser printer a few years ago. Laser printers use toner, like that used in photocopiers, and they require black, cyan, magenta and yellow toner. This is generally an expensive outlay at the beginning but the quality of printout on inexpensive ordinary printer paper is generally very high, the speed of printing is greater and the toner lasts much longer than equivalent ink-jet cartridges.

Whatever type of graphics package you use, a lot of memory is required both for storing the image and for manipulating it. Often you will want to use a scanner to transfer children's artwork from a more traditional medium to a digital format for further manipulation. This will require you to consider the best form of memory storage to allow you to transfer data. The range of devices has increased considerably of late. Many computers now come with a CD writer as standard. This means that you can save up to 600 megabytes of images on to a CD-ROM. Memory keys are solid state memory devices that plug into a computer's USB port. They can be used exactly like floppy disks – files can be copied and erased – but a typical one of 256 megabytes capacity stores more than 180 times the information that can be stored on a 1.4 megabyte floppy disk.

If your school has a full network then all files can be saved on the large server, which will have considerable hard disk storage, and can easily be picked up by any of the computers on the network. A direct cable connection, with appropriate software, can be useful to access particular files, most commonly used to download files produced on a notebook computer on to a desktop machine. Whenever you are working with graphics that are stored on floppy disk, make sure you copy it to the hard disk before you start working with it. During your activity, keep saving it to hard disk, and only at the end do a final copy to floppy disk for portability. If you continually work with a file that is only stored on floppy disk the reading and writing to disk that the computer will undertake will be extremely slow, and again the activity will become extremely frustrating. A computer can read and write to a hard disk much more quickly than it can to a floppy – technically, it has a much faster access time.

The machine that is going to manipulate the image needs not only a lot of hard disk storage but also a lot of random access memory (RAM), because the image has got to be held in memory while it is being worked on. Because of the high memory requirements, the computer program may run extremely slowly, which can be frustrating to children, who end up frantically clicking on the mouse, and causing many unexpected effects to occur consequently. In summary, if you use a computer for image manipulation it needs to be a high-specification machine, with a fast processor, large amounts of memory and an extremely large hard disk. Without this you will still be able to use paint and draw programs, but the more sophisticated activities will be frustratingly slow or impossible.

Many drawings and cartoons are available in clip art collections. These are all copyright free and can be included in any document that you wish. Clip art pictures are generally draw objects rather than paint objects, so they can be edited using a draw package. Children should be encouraged to use this editing facility as they progress through their primary education. Teachers should beware of children's overreliance on clip art products and their indiscriminate use. The ease with which images can be imported into publications should be mediated by an understanding by the children of the appropriateness of their use. There must also be

FIGURE 5.10 Editing clip art enables you to change colours and exchange elements so that the image is customised to your individual requirements

plenty of encouragement for children to create their own original work using paint and draw packages.

An important word of warning is that these packages do not make it easier to draw than when using traditional media – in fact in some cases, particularly when using a mouse, it is a much more difficult skill. As a teacher you must have very clear ideas about why a child might want to do a drawing using a paint or draw package as opposed to using pencil, crayon, pastel or paint. Use the power of the computer because it is appropriate, not simply because it is there. A child could draw a design using traditional media then scan it in to a paint package, and by using a series of tools to flip and rotate their own image, design a piece of wrapping paper that can actually be used to wrap up a Christmas present. Avoid situations where you look at an original piece of children's artwork, give the child feedback and then suggest that the child replicates it on the computer. The overriding question you, as a teacher, must ask is: why am I asking the child to do that? Giving children practice at using a different kind of program is a far from satisfactory answer.

Paint and drawing programs come in many different forms, many of them focusing on making particular tasks much easier. Computer-aided design (CAD) programs are draw packages that allow different views of the same object to be linked together, sometimes also giving a three-dimensional view of what the finished product would look like. Other specialist draw programs can be used for circuit and printed circuit board design and room layout and planning. There are other specialist paint programs (such as Paint Shop Pro or Photoshop Elements) that concentrate on making alterations to existing photographs rather than producing your own drawings. In order to avoid confusion between the two general types it is useful to talk with the children about the advantages and disadvantages of each approach throughout their time in primary school.

Main teaching and learning issues

■ Make children aware of the difference between paint and draw packages.

■ Give them opportunities to develop their technical skills of scanning and enhancing images.

■ Let children edit clip art images in order to customise them to their own requirements.

Avoid

■ Devaluing artwork in more traditional media.

■ The overuse of irrelevant clip art.

Sound packages

There are very many sophisticated sound packages available, but the ones most suitable for initial primary school work are generally quite straightforward. You can make a choice of particular types of sound (in the same way that you would choose a particular colour in a paint package) and then place a marker on to a simulation of a musical stave on the screen. The marker can be altered in length in order to make the note shorter or longer. Essentially, you simulate putting notes on a stave and, when you have completed the section, you can play back the music. A program of this nature allows for considerable experimentation, until the child is happy with the overall effect. More sophisticated effects can be achieved by playing back a number of sounds from different musical instruments at the same time.

It is possible to link electronic keyboards to computers using a midi connection, and this will allow compositions played on the keyboard to be recorded on a computer, then manipulated electronically, perhaps by cutting and pasting sections, and then playing it back through the keyboard from the computer. Software also exists that prints out music, after you have played in the notes through a keyboard.

Many computers come with simple sound software already installed, allowing you to record your voice or music and then to play it back, after effects have been added. With the increased power of computers they can now be used, as they are in professional broadcasting, as a digital tape recorder on which sounds and music can be edited together. Even quite sophisticated software is now available free from websites. This allows you to mix recorded sounds as you would in a recording studio. If you have access to a minidisc recorder good quality on-location recordings can be made that can then be downloaded on to the computer disk.

Many children might already be familiar with the use of MP3 files for playing back music. This would be a good opportunity to identify the legalities behind recording music from the Internet.

Main teaching and learning issues

- Use the software mainly for manipulating sounds.

- Make sure there is a clear focus for the manipulation or construction of the musical sounds.

Avoid

- Using a computer at the expense of traditional musical instruments.

Desktop publishing

Desktop publishing (DTP) programs allow you to manipulate text, graphic elements (lines, shading, boxes), drawings and photographs and arrange them on a page with the aim of producing a well designed piece of work. As the range of facilities within traditional word processing programs has increased, they are able to do many of the things that purpose designed desktop publishing packages can do. However, DTP does involve a different way of working and it is therefore this process that would be the main teaching outcome when deciding to introduce children to a desktop publishing program.

You should really think of desktop publishing as a page layout package. Imagine you have a sheet of paper on which you want to create a small newsheet. The sheet might well have a large title, a logo, a photograph and two blocks of text. You have all these elements available, so you would cut them out and then paste them into position on your sheet of paper – the original cut and paste method. But then you discover that the way you have typed in your text does not quite fit, and the photograph is slightly too large. So this is where the power of a desktop publishing package comes in. If the text and photograph are stored electronically and placed on the electronic sheet of paper within the DTP package then it is very easy to make the photograph slightly smaller and to decrease the size of the text (font size), or the space between lines of text (leading, pronounced 'ledding'), so that all the words fit in. The other major benefit of desktop publishing is the ability to link text from one page to another. Newspapers often start a story on page 1 and then continue it on some other page. One approach to doing this would be to cut your article into two, pasting the first part on page 1 and the second half on page 4. But as you come to rearrange the front page you notice that now there is actually room for a bit more of the text. This would now entail going to page 4, cutting a bit off the page and pasting it back on page 1. Did you take the right amount, or are you still a little short?

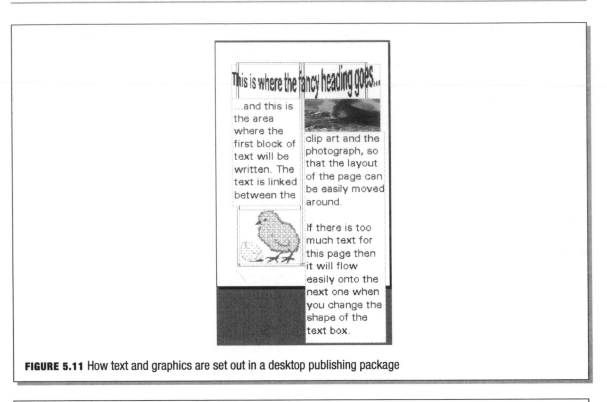

FIGURE 5.11 How text and graphics are set out in a desktop publishing package

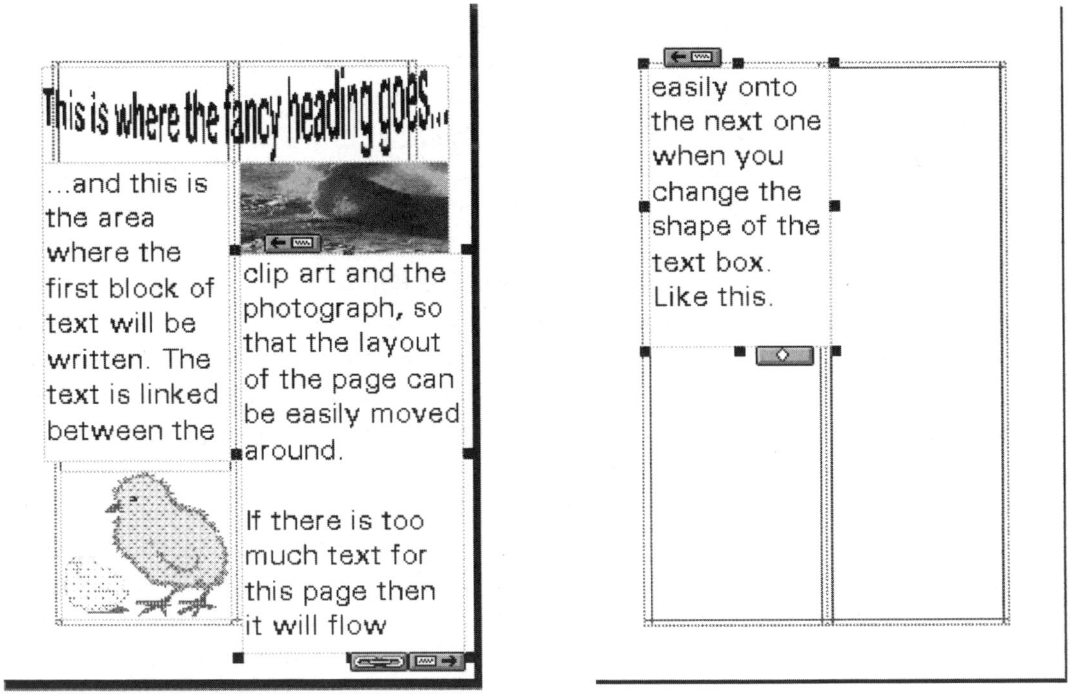

FIGURE 5.12 How text is linked between pages 1 and 2 in desktop publishing

The power of desktop publishing allows you to link the text from pages 1 to 4 automatically using text frames. The text is stored on the page in a text frame. If you make the text frame slightly smaller, less text is shown on the page, but the text has not disappeared – it is stored. When you return to page 4, you find the text in place once more.

Most desktop publishing packages now come with a wide range of suggested layouts – you just have to import the text and pictures. As an introductory exercise this is appropriate, but children must be encouraged to change these templates, or even start from scratch with a blank sheet, if the creativity that these programs allow is not to be lost.

Main teaching and learning issues

- Desktop publishing is a way of laying out a page with text blocks, borders, shading, illustrations and photographs – a wide range of technical skills need to be developed.

- All the text should be typed into a word processor and saved as a file.

- All the graphics should be worked on in draw or paint packages and then saved as a file.

- Children should start DTP work by using the suggested page designs, which are stored as templates or wizards in many packages.

Avoid

- Typing in text to a DTP package as if it were a word processor.

- Using too many different fonts in one piece of work (you can always tell when someone produces their first piece of DTP material – it contains so many different type sizes and styles).

Multimedia authoring

Multimedia authoring has been brought about because of the facilities that are now readily available on computers – a sound card, a CD-ROM rewritable drive, a high resolution screen, fast processing of information and large storage devices – and because a great deal of the multimedia material that is currently available on CD-ROM and the Internet has provided us with examples of what we could perhaps produce.

Multimedia authoring can really be thought of as an extension to desktop publishing: producing screen-based information as opposed to paper-based material and hence using the sound and moving image facilities that the computer affords us. The most common application that can be used for this is Microsoft PowerPoint, and over the past few years it has become very common for children to produce their own PowerPoint presentations.

There are a number of features that make PowerPoint or similar programs so attractive to children. It is relatively easy to incorporate good-quality photographs from a digital camera into a presentation and for this to be displayed on a large TV monitor or screen using a data

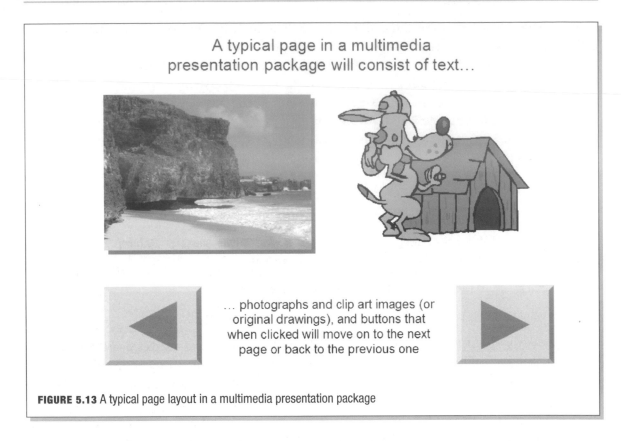

A typical page in a multimedia
presentation package will consist of text...

... photographs and clip art images (or
original drawings), and buttons that
when clicked will move on to the next
page or back to the previous one

FIGURE 5.13 A typical page layout in a multimedia presentation package

projector. Children can also select relevant clip art and add sound effects, which they could quite possibly record themselves. Together with the fact that all elements of a PowerPoint slide can be animated, this creates a much more enjoyable authoring environment than a pen and paper. But it is essential that children are taught that the reason behind any PowerPoint presentation is to communicate information and that certain types of PowerPoint presentations do not enhance communication at all.

Use of this type of presentation program also allows for greater flexibility in structuring written material. If you look through a book, you are likely to start at the beginning and read through to the end. If you find information that you feel is irrelevant, you can skip through those pages, but you are still taking very much a linear approach.

With this sort of program your document can have a branching rather than linear structure. Having digested a screenful of information, you may be given a choice of routes to follow. By clicking on one of a number of buttons, you are in control. You do not have to skim through pages of material that you know is irrelevant – you, in fact, never see it. This approach clearly also has dangers, but it is an important element in the production of multimedia products.

The audience is an important feature of any writing, but in multimedia, when there is also the requirement for the reader to have access to an expensive computer, it is even more important. If the material is designed for reception age children, have they got the technical skills to work their way through the material? If it is for parents, how can they be sure that they will actually be able to access it?

It needs to be said that the production of material of this type is extremely time-consuming and requires considerable technical skill in order to produce high-quality products. Again, there must be a reason for producing a piece of work of this nature. Without a purpose it becomes a time-consuming, pointless exercise, getting children to practise particular skills for no purpose, other than to satisfy the National Curriculum ICT requirements.

Projects of this type would consist of a background, a photograph or drawing and an area of the screen identified as a 'button', which, when clicked with the mouse, will reveal further information. The page also requires navigation controls to allow the user to move from one page to the next, return to previous pages if they wish or to leave the program completely. A simple example of a multimedia product that could realistically be achieved in the classroom is a package about the children themselves. Each page could be constructed by the children, including a scanned in photograph of themselves, some general information about them-selves in a datafile format and a favourite joke of theirs, whose punchline is revealed when you click on a particular button. The purpose would be for members of the class to know a little more about each other, and they would have practised some quite complex technical skills of importing photographs and creating buttons. It could even be envisaged that each class in a school did the same, so that information about all the children could be available to everyone else in the school. The idea could be developed further by including pictures of the children when they were very young on the front page; on clicking on a picture you go straight to the page of that particular child. Each page could also have the child's favourite piece of poetry being read by himself or herself and his or her illustration of that poem.

Multimedia authoring gives many opportunities for children's work to be used subse-quently as background research by other groups of children, emphasising the relevance of the activity – the package will actually be used.

Web authoring

Much software currently available allows its output to be presented as a web page. This is certainly the case with programs such as Microsoft Word or PowerPoint. There are also a number of automated websites that allow children to send work in for it to be displayed to a worldwide audience. The Tesco SchoolNet2000 project was one such initiative.

Although producing web pages is not a particularly common primary school activity at the moment, it is becoming something that children can do quite easily. It allows children to distribute their work to a potentially massive worldwide audience, but care must therefore be taken to ensure that only material that the school is happy to link its name to is included. While children should clearly be able to produce their own web pages, there must be a clear procedure set up for checking the material before it is made available on the Internet.

Main teaching and learning issues

- The difference between linear and branching structures.

- Multimedia authoring really needs to be a group activity.

- Quality, meaningful products require considerable planning.

- Ensure progression in technical skill is build into subsequent projects.

Avoid

- Every project requiring the class to produce a PowerPoint presentation.

Digital video

Children are familiar with the use of moving digital images on television and on computer games, and as equipment becomes readily available there are opportunities to let children experiment with using this medium. Many digital still cameras are able to produce short sections of video as well, and there is software downloadable for free from the Internet that is able to edit together video shots on a computer.

Because of its relative simplicity, compared with even a few years ago, and the fairly minimal costs involved, primary children can easily be encouraged to put together short digital videos, rather than, for example, being asked to produce two pages of writing, as a means of recording some aspect of their work. Some of the software available will join the individual pieces of video together automatically, including transitions and even sound, but the real power of opportunities like this is that they offer children the opportunity to be creative.

It is possible to include short video extracts in PowerPoint presentations, so a 30-second interview with a visitor to the school, or a panoramic shot of the front of the school incorporated into an appropriate presentation, might be a good starting point, before the children go on to produce their own epic.

Main teaching and learning issues

- This exploits the enthusiasm and interest children may have in a medium with which they are very familiar.

- Gradually introduce children to appropriate skills over a period of time.

- Start with small clips integrated into their other work, before making a major blockbuster.

Avoid

- Not letting children have a go because you think it will take too long.

Sensing and measurement

One question that might be asked is: why do we use a £700 computer to measure temperature when we could use a £2 thermometer? In many ways this is a very important question. Children should not get the idea that a computer should be used to do everything. They should be encouraged to think about the appropriateness of the equipment that they are using. But where a computer can be used to great effect is when the data can be collected over a much longer period than would be reasonable, e.g. overnight, or where lots of readings can be taken in a very short time, where the information can be very quickly and effectively displayed, and where the data can be analysed and compared.

Young children are in a position to analyse graphical representation of data that they have collected, even though they would be unable to produce the graphs themselves. The computer allows us to change the teaching strategy: the analysis of graphical data, followed by the technical production of graphs by hand, with a clearer understanding of why graphs are useful.

The simplest of experiments can easily be used to help children to relate a series of measurements to a graphical representation of the data. A temperature sensor could be left outside the classroom window and the computer set to record the temperature every ten minutes for a 24-hour period. The graph, which can be instantly produced, can be used to discuss changes of temperature during the day, the differences between day and night temperatures, and how the graph might be different on a day in December and on one in July.

Main teaching and learning issues

■ Analysis of graphical data can be introduced early in primary schools.

■ Children should be aware of the situations when this sort of approach is appropriate.

Avoid

■ Always using the computer to measure temperature.

Control

Most children's first experience of control will be when they use a floor robot. This can be made to travel forwards and backwards and to turn left and right by being given simple instructions such as 'Forward 10' or 'Turn Right'. Once children are familiar with the idea that they can control a vehicle by using simple instructions, they need to link the instructions together in sequences. For example, 'Forward 10; Turn Right; Forward 10; Turn Right; Forward 10; Turn Right; Forward 10; Turn Right' will produce a square, with each side being 10 units long.

It is now possible to develop this approach using a screen-based robot or turtle. The turtle draws the shapes on the screen as it moves, following the particular commands given. The next stage in programming, which is what this activity actually is, is to identify instructions that can be grouped together in what is called a *procedure*. In this simple example the procedure might be called *Side* and be made up of 'Forward 10; Turn Right'. To draw a square now only requires a command such as 'Side 4', which repeats the *Side* procedure four times.

Programs of this type do not only draw shapes, but can also be used to control a number of switches. The switches can be on or off, and they can be controlled for very precise periods of time. The switches are attached to an interface that changes the messages from the computer, in the form of very small electrical signals, into much larger amounts of electric current that can be used to control lamps, buzzers and motors.

A further sophistication is in the way that the computer can react to signals from the environment. We can use the ubiquitous example of traffic lights to show what teaching and learning can take place through the concept of control. A simple circuit and red, amber and green lamps can easily be operated by hand to simulate the pattern of traffic lights. But in a real-life situation you need another set of traffic lights at right angles to the first set, and the pattern of these lights must be carefully coordinated with that of the first set. It is getting a bit more difficult to organise this physically now, and remember that this pattern needs to take place 24 hours a day. This is obviously a role for a computer.

We also know that, particularly at night when the traffic flow is much less, we need the lights on one set of lights to allow free flow of traffic until a vehicle needs to pass along the less busy road. Therefore, we need a detector in the road that will know when a car is waiting to cross, and will cause the traffic lights to go through a complete cycle. So computers are very good at doing repetitive things. Children are introduced to the idea of control very much earlier in their school life when they use programmable vehicles. This exercise uses exactly the same principle, with the programmable vehicle switching motors on and off in order to make its way through a maze.

Main teaching and learning issues

- By giving very clear instructions, children are able to move floor robots.

- Screen-based turtle graphics programs introduce children to ideas of programming.

- When used with external models, control is just an automatic way of controlling switches.

- This is a very important element in much of industry today.

Avoid

- Complicating the concepts with too much wire and gadgetry.

Framework programs

Imagine a central blank screen and a selection of pictures surrounding it. By clicking on a picture you can move it and place it anywhere on the screen, fixing it in place with a further click of the mouse. This is the concept behind framework programs, which can be thought of as electronic 'fuzzy felt'. One frequently used package provides a map of the United Kingdom and a selection of weather symbols. Children can easily make up their own weather map without having to produce their own symbols using a paint package.

Once you have a copy of the framework program, which has no content, you purchase individual add-ons, which consist of a background and a selection of graphic images that you can place on the screen. The basic program also allows you to rotate and flip images, and to change their size. A program of this type is incredibly flexible. Young children can use them to create their own illustrations of traditional stories, and older children can investigate mathematical concepts or be introduced to simple computer-aided design. The program effectively is a limited drawing or paint program with integral clip art, and as such provides an excellent introduction to using these types of packages. It is also a motivating way for young children to develop mouse skills.

Remember, however, that you can do nothing with the framework program itself – you need to buy the add-on packages of backgrounds and graphics. We look at some of these packages in more detail in later chapters, as they are applicable to particular subject areas.

FIGURE 5.14 A typical layout in a framework program (Getting Dressed, from Inclusive Technology)

Main teaching and learning issues

■ These are very effective for developing mouse skills with young children.

■ They provide a good foundation to more sophisticated paint and drawing packages.

Avoid

■ Using these all the time rather than giving children more freedom with completely content-free programs.

The Computer in Control of the Child

In Chapter 5 we saw ways in which children can have control over the work that they do on a computer. Increasingly, however, there are becoming many ways in which the computer can exert control over the child. From the first time a youngster enters school, a computer will be involved in putting together the Foundation Stage profile. Subsequently, it will store all the data about the child's progress, building up a comprehensive dossier of achievement – or lack of it. The information stored will be manipulated and analysed to inform the planning of future activities, to provide parents with detailed progress reports of their child and to provide the data for the school league tables. Increasingly, the computer will be monitoring children's understanding and automatically providing new learning opportunities matched exactly to their requirements. How have we arrived at this position?

How have teaching machines evolved?

In the 1960s, particularly in the USA, there was a great movement towards programmed learning. Based on the work of the behaviourist B. F. Skinner, it worked on the principle that you identified very clear behavioural objectives, i.e. things that could clearly be measured for a particular piece of teaching. You then devised a series of activities that would help children to learn about these things and finally you would know that the teaching had been successful if the children were able to show that they could achieve these learning outcomes. This idea led to the proposition that a machine could be used to take the children through the stages that were necessary in order to complete the objectives satisfactorily. This led to the development of the sort of books that gave you some information, and then asked a question. Depending on which answer you gave, you turned to a different page. If the answer you chose was wrong, you would be given an explanation and asked a further question, the answers to which would take you to further pages in the book.

The basic concept was that if you clearly understood the idea you would quickly delve more deeply into the work. If you were having a problem, the material would provide you with more help and take you on a different route through the book. However, this was all paper-based, and as a series of questions and answers were not particularly stimulating or exciting for children, this approach did not have a great impact on mainstream teaching.

This was a first attempt to get away from a linear teaching approach. You no longer had to start at page 1 and work your way to page 300 when another route might have been more appropriate. Then, as the personal computer developed, hypertext was introduced. A screen of information appears on your computer and you are then asked to respond in some way to what you read by clicking on one of a number of buttons. You then receive a further 'page' of information on screen, which directly relates to your response – praise if you were correct, for example, or a detailed explanation and further support material if you were wrong. But was this really an appropriate use of an expensive computer: screen after screen of text-based information, which inevitably meant that the user needed to use the material in a particular location and at a particular time, perhaps having to wait until a computer was free anyway? Would a £5 paperback, with its total portability and ease of use, not have been a much more cost-effective way of learning about this particular topic? It is difficult to browse through pages on your PC while having a bath!

The technology developed, and there were opportunities for simple graphics to be incorporated into the pages, and then colour computer screens became the norm. But an equivalent paper-based product might still only cost £15. In truth, there was still little to be gained in teaching and learning terms by using a computer.

Then the technology developed further still, and the processor in a computer got faster, and hard disk storage capacities became much larger and cheaper, and the computer became multimedia, meaning that it could play sounds and show animations and video clips, and the CD-ROM (or even DVD) could now be used to store data: 700 megabytes compared with the traditional floppy disk storage of 1.4 megabytes. Now we have a machine that is no longer limited to text. Each page can incorporate audio explanations, sound effects and pictures and perhaps an animation or a video clip. We have now reached the stage where there is no cheaper alternative to using a computer for a learning package of this type.

In what ways are today's programs different from the original computer-based learning packages?

One of the features that characterised the first educational software was that it was all about 'skill and drill'. A computer is very good at matching the string of letters or numbers that you type in with a string of characters it has stored in a program. Spell 'cat'. If you typed in 'cat' you were right. If you typed in 'cta' you were wrong. If you typed in 'Cat' – well, it depended on the quality of the computer programming what response you got. Mathematical questions could be set, and only the prescribed answer was acceptable: is 5 correct but 5.00 wrong? Moreover, they could not be set out in any format that actually assisted the children to solve the problems. In the early 1980s computer-based learning was all very clever, but not particularly exciting. Not that I should be overly critical, in that we were probably, even then, stretching the computer's capabilities to the limit. A typical machine would have 16 kilobytes bytes of memory (currently machines will have 256 megabytes bytes of memory as standard), a black and white monitor and a cassette tape recorder to load the programs on the computer from short cassette tapes. By the time the program had loaded – probably at the third attempt – the lesson was over.

The problem with good computer-based learning packages is that to be effective they need to be motivating, and to be motivating they need to compare favourably with other media in the children's lives, in particular terrestrial, satellite and cable television, and video and computer games. This visual impact requires a great deal of data, which needs to be stored, and the 1.4 megabyte floppy disks that rapidly became the main source of storage were not up to it. Rapidly changing visual images, animations and perhaps video clips will only work if there is rapid access from the processor to the data on disk. A new storage medium was therefore required and development of the existing audio compact disk led to the introduction of the CD-ROM. Now we had a storage capacity of 800 megabytes, which was enough for a while, but the access times were still a little slow, causing animations to be jerky and movement from page to page to be rather slow. This led to computers spinning the CD disk much faster than it was traditionally spun for audio use, perhaps 12 times or 24 times faster. And now digital versatile disks (DVDs) are available and hold even more data.

Technically, we now have the storage capacity and processor power to produce educational computer-based learning software that is highly graphical and interactive. But there are still problems. The cost of developing highly sophisticated multimedia educational products of a standard equivalent to the games that are available is astronomical. Games, for example, are written by enormous teams of people, with widely varying expertise, more reminiscent of a blockbuster film than a piece of software. Games manufacturers can, however, get their money back many times over because of worldwide home sales – as they are very visual products the language content is usually minimal so the same product can be sold in many countries. The educational software market in any one country is not large enough to sustain economic sales, so many products will be aimed at the home first, with a subsidiary role in education.

Are content-rich multimedia CD-ROMs actually computer-based learning packages?

The true multimedia packages are not, first and foremost, designed with teaching objectives and lesson outcomes in mind. They are, indeed, not computer-learning packages – just sources of information in a multimedia format. They are designed to appeal to a wide cross-section of the software buying public, and this is a market that has increased considerably.

They can provide children with a very rich source of information, but it is unwise to get carried away and to think that the ICT approach is always best. Let us consider two very old products. The first is a CD-ROM about musical instruments. It achieves something that would be impossible to achieve without having a wide range of instruments available in the classroom, together with experienced musicians capable of playing them all – singly and together. It is also simple to use and has a very straightforward structure. You can find information easily and make effective use of it. It really makes the most of the multimedia environment.

Compare this with the second example, one of an increasing range of collections of paintings on CD-ROM. By clicking on small images of each painting you get a full screen image of it. There is also text-based information about each work of art. Why is this approach a more effective one than having all the paintings available in a high-quality book with a good contents and index. The latter would be more portable, more easily accessible and considerably cheaper when you consider that you need a multimedia computer in order to see the images.

But the home market can influence software suppliers to education's advantage. For example, one of the most common CD-ROM based encyclopaedias used in schools in the UK originally had a very American flavour (or should I say flavor) to it. Subsequent editions were expected to sell so well that the developer has been able to develop a customised version that now relates much more closely to British culture. Written materials, designed specifically for schools, have also been produced, and offer ideas for the use of these products in educational contexts, but they are not an integral part of the product.

What are current computer-based learning packages like?

Effective, high-quality, standalone, multimedia computer-aided learning material is in short supply and still focuses upon 'skill and drill' type activity. We are asking questions because they are easy for a computer to check rather than because they are meaningful questions. Basic mathematical skills such as addition cannot have alternative answers. A click on the mouse button in the appropriate place is all that is required. And perhaps this is a useful tool that can be used effectively to enhance the teaching of numeracy and literacy.

That is not to say that there have not been valiant attempts to try to change this. More sophisticated 'problem-solving' activities or puzzles are included in some packages, but then there are dangers if children are not given strategies to assist them in solving them. At a recent ICT exhibition, a child was demonstrating to me how a particular balancing problem worked. The see-saw had to be balanced by the addition of particular loads at various positions on both sides of the balance point. It had all that you might ask for in terms of quality of graphics, sound and animation and it technically worked well. However, the strategy that the child was using could be described as no more than 'trial and error'. The ease with which the 'loads' could be lifted and moved using the mouse militated against a thoughtful approach to the problem. The problem was eventually solved, but what learning had been developed? This highlights once again the importance of intervention by the teacher to structure the learning that is taking place, whether it is when reading, writing, drawing, discussing or using a computer.

What are integrated learning systems?

Programmed learning came back into the picture in a big way in the late 1990s under the guise of integrated learning systems (ILSs). An ILS is made up of the content, a system for recording individual responses and a management system. The content in most ILSs relates to numeracy and literacy skills, where the work can be arranged hierarchically. Children work in front of the machines alone, with headphones on. It is a very solitary activity.

The power of multimedia computers means that the information provided to children on screen can be exciting, motivating and educational. The same basic approaches apply, in that some information is given, some questions are asked, the child responds and then is given some feedback based on that response. The ILSs, however, also manage the learning that goes on. If a child, for example, goes through a series of mathematical questions, getting them all right, the management system can automatically take the child on to the next mathematical idea, occasionally slipping in a 'revision' question to make sure they have still remembered the principle. One element of boredom is immediately relieved – children do not have to complete all 20 questions in an exercise when they have understood the concept competently after completing three.

The support that the program can give to the children can also be managed. If, from their responses, it is clear that this particular area is causing them some difficulty, then much more detailed explanation can be provided. Conversely, if the idea is clearly understood, the explanations provided to the child can be much more concise, again ensuring that the teaching matches the child's learning needs very closely. What we have is an infinitely patient tutor, who is continuously monitoring the progress of the child and ensuring that the support comes in exactly the right amount and at exactly the right time. In fact, Vytgotsky's concept of the zone of proximal development fits in extremely well with the sophisticated management systems that will soon be readily available.

Do integrated learning systems work?

The NCET (now BECTa) was commissioned by the then Department for Education to evaluate ILSs and to explore their effectiveness in the UK education system. A very comprehensive account of the projects and their evaluation is to be found in Underwood and Brown (1997).

It is worth highlighting one or two of the main findings of the evaluation, particularly as they relate to primary age children, and what the research implies for the use of virtual learning environments (VLEs). Children working with mathematical content in the earliest stages of the projects maintained their initial learning gains, and this was evident both in groups that were continuing to use ILSs and in those that no longer used such systems. When the researchers looked at the progress that children made when working with the English language content, the effectiveness seemed to depend to a great extent on the quality of teacher intervention (Underwood *et al.* 1997).

It is apparent that teachers need to be fully trained in the use of an ILS for children to achieve the greatest learning gains. As they became proficient and confident in its use they began to use the significant amounts of feedback on individual children's performance to inform future practice. 'This led to a small-scale classroom trial of basic number skills, which indicates that the children using ILS have gained an automaticity of skill not achieved by their classroom peers. There are also indications of a shift in attitude as these children were willing to take more risks and tackle unfamiliar material' (Barrett and Underwood 1997).

There were also interesting results for underachievers, with the findings confirming 'a positive impact on the academic performance and behaviour patterns of most of the under-achievers examined'. While some children were beginning to become more involved in their learning outside the use of ILSs, this transfer is not automatic. Some children are not interested at all in the approach, much preferring to stay within their existing classes and undertake more traditional mathematical tasks. 'The very able and the very weak appear to benefit most from the system; the former being challenged and the latter being helped up the learning ladder' (Gardner 1997).

Work was done to see how ILSs could be used with children with special educational needs. An interesting development of this was identifying a baseline of basic ICT skills that a child would need to demonstrate before he or she would even be able to interact with the system. These skills include 'knows how to use delete and/or backspace keys to "rub out"', 'is able to transfer visual attention from keyboard to screen and back frequently' and 'understands that the whole prose passage must be read before the questions are attempted' (Lewis 1997).

The extent to which the child has to fit in to the approach decided by the computer is an important issue.

> Effective teaching is assumed to mean employing strategies which meet the needs of the student and enable students to develop transferable intellectual concepts and skills as well as social skills. If ILS is to be effective, it too must employ strategies which meet the needs of the students, rather than the student having to meet the strategies of the machine.
>
> (Rodrigues 1997)

This is not necessarily just the case for ILSs, but also that for any use of ICT in the classroom.

ILSs should be seen not as a teacher replacement, but as an additional resource that can have beneficial effects on children's literary and numeracy levels. In the USA, where these systems were initially developed, they do not appear to be eradicating numeracy and literacy problems, in part perhaps because they are viewed as 'the' way in which mathematics is taught.

Training teachers in the effective use of an ILS is seen as paramount if the best results are to be achieved. The feedback that it provides for teachers is extremely detailed and can produce a great deal of useful diagnostic information, but teachers need to know how to analyse the information in order to make best use of it. Interestingly, there is some evidence that if the system is used by pairs of children in a cooperative way, performance gains are actually enhanced. It would seem that 'scaffolding' provided by both a colleague and a machine is better than that provided by a machine alone.

The use of ILSs has not seen the growth that five years ago we might have imagined. Cost and effectiveness may have been the main reasons, but perhaps they have been overtaken by the concept of e-learning.

What is e-learning?

The prefacing of words with the letter 'e' seems to be becoming rather a common phenomenon. The current buzz word must be e-learning, which is short for electronic learning. This is based on the idea that learning material can be distributed over an electronic computer network and delivered to individual computer screens, although the current government's definition implies that it is synonymous with using ICT to enhance any aspect of teaching and learning.

To manage this on-line way of working, VLEs and managed learning environments (MLEs) are currently being developed. An MLE is a combination of a VLE and an information management system (IMS), so that pupil data from the IMS can be imported into the VLE and assessment and other information can be automatically transferred from the VLE to the IMS.

A VLE is a container for a whole wealth of on-line content, as well as some integrated learning tools such as e-mail, calendars and on-line notice boards. There is a vision that children will be able to access materials that will teach them everything they need to know by logging on to a VLE. What is more, they will be able to choose learning materials that focus upon their particular learning style. They will also be able to access this material from anywhere at any time, and they will be able to discuss their work 'virtually' through on-line discussion groups, sending their work electronically, via the system's internal e-mail system, to their teacher.

This approach could have very many advantages, making children more independent in their learning, and teachers would not have to spend so much time creating individual resources, knowing that children would have a wealth of learning materials that they could freely call upon. Teachers could then spend quality time concentrating on supporting the work of children on a one-to-one basis. The problem with this vision is how vastly different it is from the ways in which most primary schools currently work. The management of this type of change is a task of gigantic proportions.

The development of VLEs for primary use is generally very embryonic, but for a VLE to be effective it needs digital content, and this is currently being produced and made available through the Curriculum Online website. To get the digital content market moving, the government has provided large sums of money in the form of e-learning credits that can only be spent on digital content; the sort of learning materials that could be used with a VLE, although clearly it is also useful when used in other, more traditional, learning contexts.

There are, however, a number of challenges involved in the production of this digital content. In the main, publishers are creating text on screen rather than true effective on-screen learning materials. The reason is clear. E-learning credits cannot be used on books but they can be used on digital content. Publish the book as a text file and you have increased your market. Digital learning material is also extremely costly to produce, if indeed there are enough people who are able to write it or even understand what it really is.

So when you are evaluating digital content consider, first, if it is likely to enhance the teaching and learning of that particular topic, and, second, if it makes use of some feature of ICT that makes the resource better than it might have been if produced in a more traditional medium, such as text or video. For example, Espresso, an on-line resource incorporating on-screen interactive activities and a large number of relevant video clips linked to the primary National Curriculum, would score highly on these criteria, as would PrimaryViewPoint, a PowerPoint-based resource designed specifically as a digital resource, which provides clear structured illustrations and animations linked closely to the QCA scheme of work for science. Any resource that you find yourself reading from the screen for page upon page, and that leaves you wondering why it isn't printed out, probably fails to satisfy the criteria.

Can we write children's reports using ICT?

It is now possible to automate the process of report production by using a computer. There is a great deal of discussion about the advantages and disadvantages of such an approach. There is a view that a computer-generated report can be impersonal, and parents like to think that their child is known as a person by teachers within the school. However, the reports that can be produced can be far more detailed than it would be possible to be if they were all hand-written by staff. The process entails writing a bank of statements in a particular format, so that it is possible that they can be linked together, incorporating the child's name so that they read well. The time-consuming element is initially in the production of the bank of statements. If we just consider the ICT element of the report, then clearly we need to have statements about competence in all the strands of ICT, and about their general attitudes and level of motivation. Each statement is given a code, and then as a teacher you fill in an optical mark reader (OMR) form for each child, identifying which statements you want in this child's report. The rest of the process is an administrative task, with the OMR form being fed into a computer and the individual reports being printed. However, it is likely that they will need to be checked before being sent out to parents, with alterations being made.

There are some distinct disadvantages. Because you can give a lot of detail about the work the children are undertaking, you may produce much longer reports than you might have done traditionally, providing more information than parents actually want. There is also a danger that, for children who change little from year to year, in that they are always making excellent progress and working hard, their reports will be very similar, if not identical, from year to year, so it is probably sensible to include a different set of statements for each year that make general comments in the context of that particular year's work and topics. This, however, makes extra work in writing a new bank of statements for each year, and if topics change from year to year then so must the bank of statements.

There must be a compromise situation between the handwritten 'ICT – very good', next to one-line comments for all the rest of the curriculum subjects that tell parents very little, and the computer-generated A4 sheet for every subject, which many parents may not bother to read because it is not specific enough. Perhaps a one or two sides of A4 format, with small computer-generated paragraphs about each subject and with a handwritten comment by the class teacher would be an appropriate solution.

It is important to consider why you might consider using ICT to produce children's reports. One of the main purposes of using ICT in the management of schools must be efficiency. Is it really an efficient use of teachers' time to handwrite or type detailed reports when a computer system could perhaps produce more detailed advice for parents, making more use of administrative staff and less of teachers? However, the teachers will clearly be heavily involved in the production of the bank of statements in the first place, and there must really be different banks for each year, as otherwise children may well get similar, if not identical, reports from year to year.

Main teaching and learning issues

- The computer is an extremely powerful tool – make sure you understand, and make the most of, its power, and use it to enhance children's learning experiences.

- Be aware of the differing roles that a computer can have.

- Use a computer where it can save time and money, provided it can enhance the provision.

- The introduction of a VLE is a major whole-school teaching and learning development, not something that can be done in a piecemeal way.

Avoid

- Using a computer *solely* for 'skill and drill' activities.

ICT and the Core Subjects of the National Curriculum

This chapter provides a few ideas for incorporating ICT into your work in the National Curriculum core subjects of English, mathematics and science. The activities are designed not to be replicated in your classroom, but to provide you with a framework out of which you can develop your own activities using your own school's hardware and your preferred software. The activities are written in a very general way so that any type of software, as identified in Chapters 5 and 6, will be appropriate.

How can ICT be used specifically in English work?

One of the most important roles for ICT is in the communication and exchange of ideas, and this has a vital role in much primary work. Children presenting ideas, having identified an audience and purpose, and giving children the opportunity to decide on the best way in which to communicate them are other important elements of literacy work that ICT can support.

There are also ways in which children can exchange ideas with other children in the UK and throughout the world, and this will involve them in discussion of the disadvantages and advantages of the different media. Consideration can be given to telephone, post, electronic mail, conferencing and bulletin boards, taking into account factors such as the number of people involved, cost, distance, requirement for immediate or developed thoughtful response and whether or not the message needs to be visual.

Entitlement to ICT in Primary English (BECTa 2003b) identifies that ICT in English can help children to:

- interact with peers and other communities, access and research information and publish to real audiences worldwide;
- work in role, and engage with real-time situations that promote teamwork, citizenship, thinking skills and the choice of genre to address purpose and audience.

The emphasis on literacy has also focused upon work at word, sentence and text level. ICT strategies related to word level work include listening to single words and linking them to appropriate illustrations, phonic and word recognition programs, spelling programs and the use of spell checking facilities on word processors. At sentence level, programs are available that test children's ability to use correct punctuation and grammar in 'skill and drill' type programs. Teachers may also customise material so that children are asked to punctuate sentences that have already been input into a word processor. This will allow children to practise manoeuvring the cursor around the screen using either keyboard or a mouse, as well as developing their English sentence level skills. At text level there are activities concerning model text, which is normally seen as a big book, but equally well could be text that is shared on a large display screen or interactive whiteboard in the classroom. There are programs that are designed for cloze procedure activities, and there are more individual and open-ended activities involving children writing and editing their own textual material, and reading and interrogating other people's texts.

Using talking story CD-ROMs

There are a wide range of talking story books, many of which now originate in the UK and so have British voices and spellings. Each page usually consists of a brightly coloured picture with some animation of the characters. A few sentences of text appear and each word is highlighted as the words are spoken. Many contain a feature where clicking the mouse on particular parts of the picture makes further animations and sounds occur. You might sit with the children and listen to them repeat each sentence after it is spoken by the computer. Encourage the children to click on to particular graphic images to show them the animations and sounds that occur.

ICT teaching points

- Mouse control.

- Familiarity with interacting with a computer.

Writing about myself

Produce an overlay keyboard layout that includes all the words necessary for children to describe themselves in a number of sentences (e.g. I, am, four, five, years, old, have, green, blue, brown, eyes, fair, red, brown, black, hair). Children can then use the overlay keyboard to write sentences about themselves. When the overlay keyboard is integrated with a word-processing program, the complete words appear on the screen when the appropriate section of the overlay keyboard is pressed. Start the activity as a group discussion, finding out the words that they want to use, and then produce the overlay to match the word bank the children have devised.

Writing nursery rhymes

Produce an overlay keyboard layout for a nursery rhyme. With some overlay editors it is possible to insert pictures, as well as text, into word processors. The content of the overlay can be as simple or complex as you wish. For example, it could include all the words of one nursery rhyme, but not in the correct order, together with one appropriate illustration. In this case the activity would be an ordering one, with the children recognising the words of the rhyme and putting them in the correct order, and then incorporating an illustration. You could ask the children to use the normal keyboard to type in their name at the bottom of the piece of work, before it is printed out and displayed. At this point children should be aware that they can save their work on to floppy disks by using the *save* command, and that they can print their work using a printer connected to their computer using the *print* command.

Subsequently, children should make use of the normal computer keyboard. At this point the *delete* key should be introduced as a way of removing mistakes. They should also be shown that the *shift* key can be used to change lower case letters into upper case. The ICT skills that are being developed here are mouse control and familiarity with interacting with a computer.

Many variations of this activity are possible, so that it can be adapted for children of different abilities. The children can be helped by having a copy of the nursery rhyme in front of them. You could include the words and pictures from two nursery rhymes, so that children have to be far more careful in their selection. Some of the easier words could be missed out of the overlay so that the children have to type these in themselves, or, perhaps, if it is a very well known rhyme, they could attempt to type in the words from memory. This activity is probably best done in pairs. In some cases, some peer tutoring might be appropriate, although the children who are acting as tutors must understand that they are helping and advising their partners – not doing it for them. Alternatively, children of similar skill levels could work together, with strict guidance being given about sharing the actual time spent using the keyboard.

ICT teaching points

Mouse control.

Familiarity with interacting with a computer.

Making use of a paper keyboard

As children are introduced to using a 'real' keyboard as opposed to an overlay keyboard, the use of a paper keyboard can help to familiarise them with the layout. Produce a copy of a keyboard on cardboard for each child. Get them to colour in each function key as they are introduced to it. The keys for which this is particularly important at this level are *delete* and *shift*. Get the children to add the lower case letters to the keys for the appropriate capital letters on their chart. This reinforces learning of upper/lower case letters and gives them a useful reference tool.

The ICT skills that are being developed here are making children aware of the structure of a keyboard, and a location of a few of the important function keys.

ICT teaching points

- Location of the *delete* and *shift* keys.
- Familiarity with the layout of the computer keyboard.

Editing text

Provide the children with a short story or nursery rhyme both on paper and as a word-processed file. The computer file version should have a number of mistakes in it that the children should correct using the paper version as a reference. This is an ideal opportunity to develop children's use of the cursor keys to move around the text (up, down, left and right) as well as using the mouse, and to teach children how to use the *delete* and *backspace* keys (*delete* for removing the character in front of the flashing cursor and *backspace* for removing the character behind the cursor).

Producing name labels

Ask the children to write their name using the keyboard and a word-processing program. They should then enlarge the text size to 36 point, change the font if they wish and centre the text on the page. Then they should use a rectangle tool to draw a border around the name, and select an interesting line style. They can then choose a clip art picture and insert it at one corner of the name label. They should then save the file and print it out. They can be encouraged to use similar techniques to produce title pages for some of their work. Some children will be able to use programs that create artistic shapes for their lettering.

ICT teaching points

- Formatting using the alignment function.

- Changing font style and size.

- Producing simple shapes using drawing tools.

- Importing clip art images into the document.

Changing text

There are many opportunities for children to interact with text using a word processor. This will allow them to experiment with different forms of writing in a temporary way, and will also develop more detailed text manipulation techniques with the word processor. Give the children a narrative text and ask them to change it into a script for a radio play. This could lead them into the use of on-screen invisible tables that allow the name of the character to appear in the left hand column of the page, with their dialogue typed continuously in the larger right hand column.

A fairly short activity, which relates to the nature of words, is to give the children a piece of text and ask them to identify all the adjectives included in it. Then, using a thesaurus, they could change every adjective – first, so that the passage retains its original meaning, and, second, so that it means something completely opposite, although it still has to make sense.

Emphasising the importance of audience, children could be given the description of a holiday resort, and asked to rewrite it to appeal to young children, 18- to 25-year-olds, families, couples and elderly people. The skill in this activity is not in making things up that would appeal to the particular audience, but in using the information they have been given and emphasising what they believe to be the important features of that particular target group.

ICT teaching points

- Formatting the page for a script using invisible tables.

- Developing expertise with spell checker and thesaurus.

- Drafting and redrafting within the word processor.

Alliteration

Make use of the facilities of a word processor to highlight particular words in alliterative sentences. The first letters of words can be made bold, italicised or given distinctive colours. Alternatively, you could make the letters bigger or more distinctive by using a different font.

ICT teaching points

- Highlighting text before attempting to change its features.

- Changing font style and size.

- Changing attributes of text to bold, italics, underlined or different colours.

Producing books for younger readers

This gives an opportunity to develop presentation skills, as well as writing original material. If a group of children work on the book, there are opportunities for collaborative writing. After an initial discussion about the basic story line and the target audience, in, say, a group of six, a pair will write the first part of the story, to be followed later by the second and third pairs, who should complete it. The group should now look at the overall story and draft and redraft it until there is consensus among the group. Each pair can now work on illustrations for the story, which could be clip art, scanned in or digitally produced photographs and drawings or original computer artwork. The group would now use a desktop publishing program to integrate the text and the graphics into a form that could be tested with younger children.

ICT teaching points

- Integration of text and graphics in a desktop publishing package.

- Drafting and redrafting of text collaboratively using a word processor.

- Use of an art package to produce original artwork or to edit clip art or scanned images.

Cloze passage

There are a number of programs that automatically produce cloze text. Children can type in a few sentences about a topic, and then get another pair to fill in the gaps that are produced by the program. This helps children in predicting which letters are most likely to appear in particular positions in words.

Class information package

The production of a class multimedia presentation is an ideal introduction to this area of work. The skills needed are generally very similar to those of desktop publishing. You should prepare a basic template with the navigation buttons and frames for text and photographs. The children should then produce their own individual page containing general information about themselves. The photograph can be one from home, which can be scanned into the computer, or it could be taken at school using a digital camera. On a second screen, each child could produce a piece of work of which he or she is particularly proud, such as a poem or a painting. All the images can then be put together into a whole package. The front page might consist of small images of everyone in the class. When you click on an image, you immediately go to that child's pages. There are many opportunities for this type of work to be extended. A sound recording of each child's voice could be incorporated, and some children might want to include more of their own work on other pages. The package could then be available at parents' evenings, or it could be available in other classrooms so that children's work can be shared and valued.

ICT teaching points

- Try to make sure there is a real purpose for the ICT products children produce.

- Use ICT to provide innovative and motivating ways for children to record their work.

Information guide for visitors to your school

Children's desktop publishing skills can be developed much further if they are encouraged to produce materials that will actually be useful. Give children the opportunity to think about the orientation and folding of the paper that could be used for a brochure and about the use of multiple columns and text wrapping around illustrations. They will also need to think of the language level for the appropriate audience. Is the material for adults, or is it for new Year 3 children on their introductory visit to the school? They will need to produce draft ideas, redraft and then proof read the material before it is finally printed. Avoid the use of 'wizards' or 'macros' to place text and graphics automatically into position on the screen. It is reasonable to use these in order to give the children some ideas about layout and design, but they should develop their own ideas, not copy other people's.

ICT teaching points

■ Children need to think carefully about the audience for their work.

■ Wizards make things technically easier but restrict children's creativity.

How can ICT be used specifically in mathematics work?

An important element of ICT in numeracy work is an understanding of how important it is to express instructions in a clear and concise way. This, in one way, illustrates the restrictive nature of computers as machines, in that they will only work when given very precise and detailed instructions. Thus there is a grammar and syntax to much work in ICT, and comparisons can be made between reasons for grammar when writing and grammar when giving a robot instructions. There is a structure to the English language so that there is a framework for communication between people. Similarly, there must be a structure so that a machine can understand what you are asking. In both cases the structure must be learned.

Much practical mathematical work can be done with floor robots, where sequencing, distance and sizes of angles are all important concepts that can be investigated in a practical way. Spreadsheets are important tools for use in mathematics, where numerical patterns can be investigated much more quickly than when using pen and paper techniques. You are able to concentrate on the patterns rather than the computational skills. There is a large number of opportunities for asking questions like 'What happens to that, if I change this?'

Entitlement to ICT in Primary Mathematics (BECTa 2003c) identifies five major opportunities where ICT can enhance children's learning in mathematics. These are:

■ learning from feedback;

■ observing patterns;

■ exploring data;

■ teaching the computer;

■ developing visual imagery.

Exploring tessellations

Use a program that can put together tiles of different shapes and colours to produce tessellated patterns. Start simply by getting the children to tessellate square tiles. Then allow them to experiment with more intricate shapes and colours. Show them how they can flip the tiles both vertically and horizontally.

Which is the most popular coloured pencil?

Ask the children to look at their collection of coloured pencils and choose the one that is their favourite. Ask each child to show you the colour he or she has chosen. Get the children to input the data into a simple database program that can show information in a graphical form. Show the children what the bar chart looks like on the screen. Discuss which is the most popular colour – the bar that is the tallest – and which is the least popular one. Finish off the activity by getting the children to bring their chosen pencils to you. Arrange them in rows. Discuss how the longest row is the same as the tallest line on the graph.

Discovering square roots

Talk to children about square numbers and square roots. Discuss the fact that $5 \times 5 = 25$ and $6 \times 6 = 36$. So the square root of 25 is 5 and the square root of 36 is 6. But what would the square root of 30 be? What number multiplied by itself would give 30? Children should then use a computer-based or hand-held calculator to experiment. They should eventually reach the point where they find that $5.4 \times 5.4 = 29.16$, but $5.5 \times 5.5 = 30.25$. So what number is between 5.4 and 5.5? This leads to a discussion about place value. With trial and error techniques they will eventually get to a figure such as 5.477225575052.

You might consider using a spreadsheet for this calculation. By putting the number in the first column and a simple formula in the top cell of the second column (=A2*A2) and then copying it down through all the cells, it is possible to type in any number in the first column and then see its square in the second one. It is also possible to see what strategy the child selected to use, and this can be discussed afterwards. It also saves having to write all the calculations down. Beware, however, that this activity can be somewhat curtailed if someone discovers the square root function on a computer or calculator.

Number	Number Squared	
5	25	
6	36	
5.5	30.25	
5.55	30.8025	
5.54	30.6916	
5.45	29.7025	
5.46	29.8116	
5.47	29.9209	
5.48	30.0304	
5.475	29.975625	
5.477	29.997529	
5.479	30.019441	
5.478	30.008484	
5.4775	30.00300625	
5.4773	30.00081529	
5.4771	29.99862441	
5.4772	29.99971984	
5.47725	30.00026756	
5.47723	30.00004847	
5.47721	29.99982938	
5.47722	29.99993893	
5.477225	29.9999937	
5.477226	30.00000466	
5.4772255	29.99999918	
5.4772257	30.00000137	
5.4772256	30.00000027	
5.47722555	29.99999973	
5.47722557	29.99999994	
5.477225575	30	

FIGURE 7.1 A simple trial and error approach to finding a square root using a spreadsheet

ICT teaching points

- Setting up a formula within a spreadsheet.

- Copying a formula to other cells.

- Formatting a spreadsheet.

Moving a floor robot

These robots come in a range of designs, but basically they consist of a vehicle that can be programmed to go forwards, backwards and turn around. At this stage the actual distances the robot travels are not really important. Descriptions such as 'a little' or 'a lot' are all that are required. This can be done as a whole class or large group activity. Put in a command to the robot, such as 'Forward 10', start the robot from a fixed position in the classroom and watch how far it goes. Return the robot to its starting position and put in the command 'Forward 5'. Get the class to predict how far it will go now. Then get children to put in the commands and stand in front of the robot just where they think it will stop. Develop this activity further with moving backwards, and then left and right. At this stage children only need to be aware that it is possible to give instructions to a robot that it will follow, and that the larger the numbers, the more it moves or turns. This activity can be combined with work on telling left from right.

Carrying a message

Once the children are familiar with the floor robot, set them the task of carrying a message from one area of the classroom to another by programming the robot.

ICT teaching points

- Introduction to simple control instructions.

- Sequencing instructions together.

Screen-based turtle

Remind children of the work they will have done with floor robots. Introduce them to a screen-based turtle program. Here they use the same ideas of 'Forward', 'Backwards', 'Right Turn' and 'Left Turn', but instead of a robot moving around the floor, a turtle-shaped object moves around the screen, leaving a trail. This means that the program can be used to draw shapes. At this stage the children should concentrate on drawing squares and rectangles. This work will give them a good understanding of the properties of shapes, e.g. in a square all the sides are the same length, and in a rectangle opposite sides are the same length.

Following a maze

Produce a maze on a piece of clear transparent film. Fix this over the monitor with a small piece of masking tape. Get the children to produce a program that will move the screen turtle from one end of the maze to the other.

ICT teaching points

- Putting instructions together into a sequence.

- Making use of procedures.

Research at the burger store

In this activity set up a spreadsheet for a fictitious burger store and ask groups of children to analyse the data by answering a series of questions. It might be possible for the children to get in touch with a local burger store to get some real data themselves. The basic spreadsheet consists of nine columns, with one for item, one for cost and one for the sales for each day of the week. The children can add formulae to the spreadsheet to find out, for example, the value of total sales in a week. The questions can range considerably in complexity. Simple questions such as 'On which day were the most cheeseburgers sold?' can lead on to things such as 'What was the daily average amount of money taken on hot drinks during the week, and how does this compare with that taken on cold drinks?', which again could be extended to consider what time of year these figures are for. The more data you include in the spreadsheet, the more opportunities the children will have to explore their own particular areas.

ICT teaching points

- Inputting information to a ready-prepared spreadsheet.

- Adding formulae to a spreadsheet.

- Using 'What would happen if . . . ?' type questions.

How can the school tuck shop make a profit?

Children should be able to construct their own spreadsheet, in most cases selecting their own fields. In this case the fields might include 'Name of item', 'Buying cost', 'Selling cost', 'Number sold', 'Number in stock', 'Total money taken' and 'Total profit'. Children could then look at ways of increasing the profit. Is it better to keep the profit small and sell more products, or increase the profit margin of the most popular items? Children are able to use the spreadsheet as a model, and can investigate the model by asking questions of the type 'What happens to the profit if I . . . ?'

ICT teaching points

■ Modelling using a spreadsheet.

■ Asking 'What would happen if . . . ?' type questions.

How can ICT be used specifically in science work?

In science you are likely to be using ICT either as a source of information or as a tool to assist with scientific investigations. There is a wealth of CD-ROM material on scientific topics, much of it highly interactive, and this can be used by children as an element of research, or, if displayed on a large screen or interactive whiteboard in the classroom, many of the excellent animations to be found on these disks can be used to illustrate a whole-class discussion instigated by the teacher.

The science section of the National Curriculum in Action website (www.ncaction.org.uk) identifies the following ways in which ICT can help children in their science work:

■ to access, select and interpret information;

■ to recognise patterns, relationships and behaviours;

■ to model, predict and hypothesise;

■ to test reliability and accuracy;

■ to review and modify their work to improve the quality;

■ to communicate with others and present information;

■ to evaluate their work;

■ to improve efficiency;

■ to be creative and take risks;

■ to gain confidence and independence.

This list is particularly useful in identifying how well a scientific investigation can successfully integrate ICT together with other activities, showing its use as a tool to assist with investigations in a wide range of ways, but not replacing the actual practical activity itself. Simulations are available, and they have their uses for activities that would be impossible to undertake practically, such as predator and prey relationships.

When you are starting out, the initial stimulus could be some research work using a presentation or a website. This could lead to the generation of a question, which may benefit from being undertaken collaboratively on a word processor, so that the group can keep changing the form of the question quite easily until they are satisfied with it. Similarly, their predicted outcomes and planning could be supported by word processing or some flow chart software. Collection of data could be done by sensors and the data could be displayed in both tabular and graphical form using database software. The support of the computer has now made it easier for the interpretation and evaluation to take place, not least because less time has to be taken on collecting the data and plotting the graphs. The emphasis is now on higher-order thinking rather than basic and repetitive data handling skills. Finally, the computer can be used by the children to communicate their findings either in print, incorporating full colour graphs, or on-screen as a presentation or multimedia package.

Computers at home

As homework, ask children to bring a list of things at home that they think are like computers or have parts of computers within them. Collate all the ideas during a class discussion and make a list of all the items that have some microelectronics in them. See if you can decide the main features of electronic devices. Many of them will have digital displays: microwaves, VCRs, alarm clocks etc.

ICT teaching points

- Awareness of the role of ICT in society.

Parts of a plant

After having discussed the parts of a plant, ask children to draw their own picture of a plant and to label each part using a paint or draw program. For children who need extra support, provide a basic outline of the plant, which they can enhance and label themselves. This idea can be adapted for various uses, e.g. naming parts of the body.

ICT teaching points

- Use of basic art package tools.

- Incorporating text.

- Simple introduction to desktop publishing.

Travelling down a ramp

Ask the children to bring in a toy vehicle from home. It must have moving wheels. Ask the children to name their vehicles. Each child then puts the vehicle at the top of a ramp and it is timed to see how long it takes to get to a fixed point on the floor. The child types the vehicle's name and the time it took to travel down the ramp (in seconds) into a spreadsheet you have already prepared. When all the class have entered their information display a bar chart to show the quickest and the slowest. Discuss the shape of the bar chart. As extension work you could develop the format of the spreadsheet so that each vehicle could have three turns and the average of the three times is shown on the bar chart. This activity ties in with work on forces in science.

ICT teaching points

- Using a ready-prepared spreadsheet.

- Using a spreadsheet because of the calculation required to find the average.

Insulation

Each group of children should do a separate experiment using a temperature sensor in a fixed quantity of ice, which is surrounded by a sample of material in an attempt to prevent the ice from melting too quickly. By using a computer sensor the group has some choice over the length of time over which the readings are taken and the gaps between individual readings. At the end of the experiment the group prints out a graph of the results and fixes a small sample of material to it for display. Subsequently, other groups of children repeat the experiment, but each time they use a different type of material. When all the groups have completed the experiment a class discussion is held about the displayed graphs. Discuss insulation and the advantages and disadvantages of using a temperature sensor for this activity compared with a thermometer.

ICT teaching points

- Setting up and using sensing software.

- Interpretation of graphical representation of data.

Using a digital microscope

The Intel digital microscope is reasonably priced and gives children an opportunity to look through a microscope without the difficulties associated with a more traditional instrument. It is plugged directly into the computer's USB socket, and the software it comes with includes some images that have been taken with the microscope, both stills and video. Children are easily able to look at any material that they are studying, such as kitchen roll to show the structure of the paper fibre and rocks to give an idea of the individual particle shape and size.

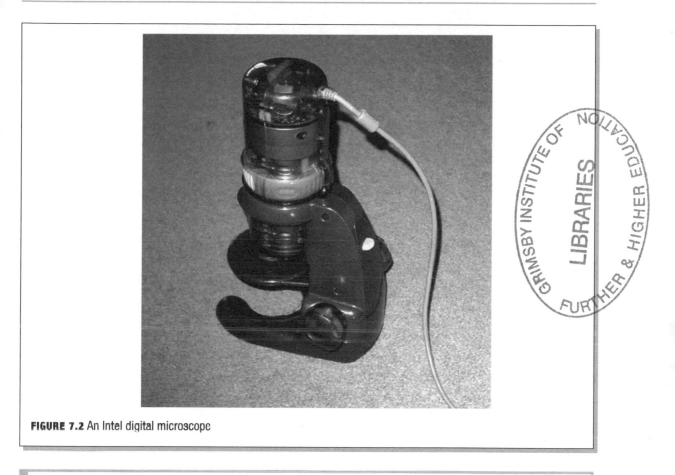

FIGURE 7.2 An Intel digital microscope

ICT teaching points

■ Using this microscope and a digital projector, the whole class can see highly magnified images 'live'.

■ This allows us to do something that without ICT would have been impossible.

Temperature map of the school

Use temperature probes connected to a computer to monitor the temperature around the school for prolonged periods. This could be part of a long-term project with each pair in the class being responsible for setting up the equipment in their selected location and monitoring the temperature changes over a 24-hour period. Clearly the locations chosen need to be secure and a notebook computer should be used, if available, so that the children can easily move the system around. Each group should produce a graph of the temperature change and stick it in the appropriate position on a large wall-mounted map of the school. When each pair has completed the task, a group discussion can be held to analyse the findings and discuss issues such as location of existing radiators, whether the heating switches on and off at the most appropriate times and ideas for conserving more heat in the buildings.

ICT teaching points

- Setting up and using sensing software.

- Interpretation of graphical representation of data.

Sensing the brightness of light from candles

As part of a science activity into light, children can use a light sensor connected to a computer to investigate the amount of light given off by a range of different candles. They would need to set the experiment up to ensure that it was conducted in a fair way, e.g. ensuring that the distance from the candle to the sensor was always the same and that the ambient light level in the room remained the same. The results would be recorded graphically using the sensing software and could be integrated into the children's word-processed account of the experiment. As extension work children could look at whether the amount of light given off depended on features such as the height, the thickness or the colour of the candle, or the original length of the wick.

ICT teaching points

- Opportunity to interpret variable light levels.

- Opportunity for detailed data analysis.

Household appliances

Building on the discussion of items in the home that have microelectronics included in them, ask pairs of children to produce their own database of household appliances. Many children will need support in the form of an outline database, but some may be able to make an attempt at devising one of their own. The sort of questions you would want answered are 'Which devices are the most common in the home?', 'Which devices are controlled electronically?' and 'Which devices need electricity in order to work?'

ICT teaching points

- Inputting data into a database.

- Formulating their own database with support.

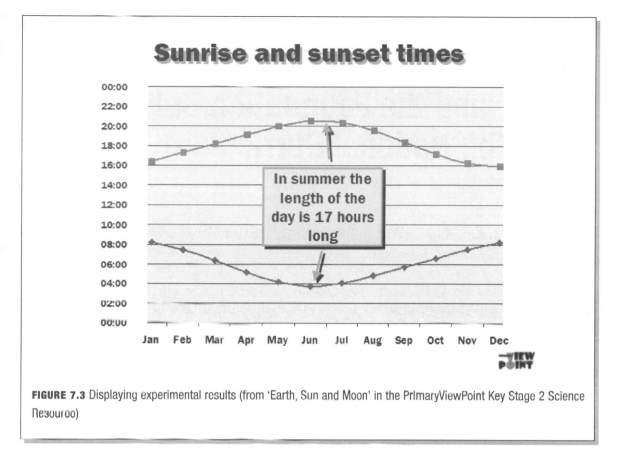

FIGURE 7.3 Displaying experimental results (from 'Earth, Sun and Moon' in the PrimaryViewPoint Key Stage 2 Science Resource)

Lengths of days

Input data about sunrise and sunset times into a spreadsheet. If you do it for a long period of time, you can then see patterns related to length of day. Plot the results graphically to show how the length of day changes throughout the year. Obtain data from another part of the world and compare the graphs you get.

This work can easily be displayed and discussed by putting the graph into a PowerPoint presentation and annotating it. Figure 7.3 shows a sample from 'Earth, Moon and Sun' (in PrimaryViewPoint 2003).

ICT teaching points

- Spreadsheets can be used to do multiple calculations very quickly.

- Analysis and interpretation of graphical data.

- Data can easily be presented on an interactive whiteboard using a PowerPoint presentation.

ICT and the Foundation Subjects of the National Curriculum

Am I using ICT to develop children's capability or to enhance teaching and learning?

Within a school, you need to do both. If children are to use ICT as a tool to enhance their own teaching and learning they clearly need to have the capability to use the ICT to its fullest extent. However, the move towards an e-learning school means that teaching and learning can be greatly enhanced by the use of ICT.

Should ICT be taught separately or as a cross-curricular activity?

The answer to this question is both! The QCA Scheme of Work for ICT gives an excellent structure for the ICT work that needs to be covered at Key Stages 1 and 2 in order to cover ICT capability.

Merely by looking at the unit titles of the ICT Scheme of Work for Key Stages 1 and 2 you can see that some fit in well with other areas of the curriculum. The challenge in your school planning is to ensure that children develop their use of ICT right across the curriculum. Anecdotal evidence over the past five years has suggested that in many schools a child's use of PowerPoint in Year 6 (and also in the secondary school) is not any more sophisticated than it might have been in Year 2.

The document *Information and Communication Technology* (QCA/DfES 2003) contains a great deal of useful information for the teaching of ICT capability in primary schools, but most significantly it identifies how the ICT Integrated Tasks from the ICT Scheme of Work can be taught as part of other elements of the National Curriculum.

Let us look in detail at one of the units, Unit 3A – Combining text and graphics, although the strategy outlined here can be used with any of the units. The unit starts off with a scene-setting activity to cover the key idea 'that text and graphics can be combined to communicate information'.

- Show the class a range of greeting cards. Discuss the designs and point out elements, such as pictures, fonts, captions and messages. Divide the class into groups and ask each group to examine one card. Ask them to produce an annotated poster identifying the card's key features.

- Look at messages and how they are written. Ask children to think about cards that they could design and produce.

The learning outcome will be 'that children recognise key features of layout'.

Then the unit identifies a series of short focused tasks, looking at the following techniques and key ideas.

Technique: to alter font type, size and colour for emphasis and effect

- Type in a number of words, e.g. 'rainbow', 'grow', 'lean', 'high', 'low', 'stairs' and 'ghost'.

- Show the class font editing features, such as how to change font type, size and colour. Ask the children to change the look of each word so that it reflects its meaning, e.g. placing each letter of 'rainbow' in a different colour, increasing the font size of each letter in 'grow'.

Learning outcome: Children will alter the look of text to create an effect

Key idea: that ICT can be used to improve text

Technique: to amend text and save changes

- Type in a piece of text using 'nice' as the only adjective.

- Remind the class how to edit text by highlighting words and over-typing them. Demonstrate how to save work and give it a sensible name. Ask the children to edit the text using more varied adjectives and to save their work.

Learning outcome: Children amend text and save their work

Technique: to combine graphics and text

- Prepare examples of text which would benefit from illustrations, e.g. a description of a pyramid. Demonstrate to the class how to locate, retrieve, insert and add a graphic into a piece of text. Show the class how to re-size a graphic so that it fits on the page. Ask the children to search a clip art file or a CD-ROM to locate graphics and copy them into a piece of text.

Learning outcome: Children combine graphics and text

Technique: to use the shift key to type characters, such as question marks

- Enter a piece of text and replace all the punctuation marks with 'x'.

- Discuss how authors use punctuation marks for effect and remind the class how to use the shift key to type upper case letters. Show them how the key can be used to type other characters.

- Ask the children to replace each 'x' with the correct punctuation. Ask them to print out their work.

Learning outcome: Children amend text using the correct key combinations

This is then followed by an 'integrated task', which should bring all the learning developed in the unit together.

■ Tell the class that they are going to produce a class magazine, which will include pictures and captions, and explain that they will use punctuation and font effects.

■ Divide the children into pairs and ask them to choose a theme for a page in the magazine. Get them to create, or capture, a picture for their page and ask them to caption the picture. Tell the children to print their work and bring the work together to form the magazine. Finally, discuss with the class the advantages of using ICT.

Information and Communication Technology (QCA/DfES 2003) provides alternative contexts for the delivery of this integrated task. Here is the task for Unit 3A with the learning objective – 'Children should learn to combine graphics and text to communicate information' – structured so that it can be linked to the Framework for Teaching English: Year 3:

Possible Teaching Activities

Explain to the children that they are going to use ICT in two different ways. First, they will work together in pairs or small groups to write a short play script for a traditional story or fable using ICT. They will follow this up by working together to produce either a programme or flyer for their play; this should include pictures and different font effects.

Ask the children to work collaboratively, sharing ideas. Encourage them to re-read what they have written, and amend it to correct errors. Discuss how some sentences could be improved. Show how a sentence can be changed without deleting it. Remind them that they should make their amends using correct key combinations, and to save their work. Encourage them to use different coloured text to highlight different characters, stage instructions, etc. Remind them to use question marks and exclamation marks appropriately.

Next, the children create their programme or flyer advertising the play. They should keep it very simple, *e.g. use only a picture and title*. Encourage them to select and insert appropriate pictures from a prepared bank of images. Children should choose appropriate font sizes, colours and styles.

Finally, discuss with the class the purposes of using ICT in the two different tasks. Discuss the advantages of using ICT to draft and redraft the script as opposed to writing out ideas by hand.

Show the class some examples of the programmes or flyers using a whiteboard or data projector, and ask children to explain their choices of font size, colour and layout. *What have they learnt? What might they do differently next time?*

Learning outcomes

Children

■ use ICT to refine and edit text;

■ combine graphics and text to produce a programme or flyer for their play;

■ show sensitivity to the needs of the audience.

Here is a different slant on the same integrated task, with the same learning objective, this time linked to science unit 3A, 'Teeth and eating':

Possible Teaching Activities

Explain to the children that they are going to produce a poster to illustrate foods for growth and foods that help us stay active. Discuss with the children what constitutes a balanced and healthy diet. Talk about the possible audience for such a poster, e.g. *Where could the poster be located? What age group might the poster be aimed at? How would this affect the content and layout? What sort of information should the poster contain?*

Ask the children to work in pairs to produce their poster. Encourage them to select and insert appropriate pictures from a prepared bank of images. Remind them to use key word searches when locating their images in the large database. Children should choose appropriate font sizes, colours and styles to convey their message. Remind them to save their work with an appropriate file name and location.

Show the class some examples of the posters using a whiteboard or data projector, and ask children to explain their choices of font size, colour and layout. *What have they learnt? What might they do differently next time?*

Learning outcomes

Children

- combine graphics and text to produce a poster identifying different food types and their effects on the body;

- show sensitivity to the needs of the audience.

This document should prove extremely useful when you are planning an integrated ICT scheme for your school.

ICT teaching points

- The ICT scheme of work concentrates on developing ICT capability.

- Integrated tasks taught in this way have both subject and ICT learning objectives.

How can ICT be used specifically in art and design work?

Entitlement to ICT in Primary Art and Design (BECTa 2003d) identifies how the use of ICT can support pupils' learning in art and design:

- by enhancing their ability to explore, develop and present ideas;
- by providing a new medium to investigate and make art and design;
- by providing a tool to evaluate and develop work;
- by providing access to a range of resources to increase pupils' knowledge and understanding of art and design.

It states that children are entitled to use ICT:

- to gain access to a wide range of knowledge and information sources;
- to gain access to a new tool/medium that can be used to develop creative ideas;
- to communicate in different ways and to receive critical feedback on their ideas;
- to consider, compare and discuss the differences and similarities in the work of artists, craftspeople and designers in different times and cultures, including the impact of digital media on contemporary art and design practice.

The use of paint and draw packages (for a discussion of the difference between the two see Chapter 5) can be developed in two ways. First, they can be used in a way that mimics the use of alternative media. The range of brushes, fill tools and spray cans simulates the painting environment, and the advantages are that changes can very easily be made and it is not as messy in the classroom. But it is a different medium, giving different outcomes. Second, there are actions that can only really be undertaken by using such packages, including cutting, copying and transformations, as well as deformations and shape changes that are possible with many programs.

There are also exciting opportunities to use digital cameras, animation programs and increasingly digital video in the primary classroom. Some schools already provide opportunities for children to experiment with these newer technologies, but others have yet to take on the challenge.

Some embryonic activities follow, which focus, in the main, on these particular areas. They should give you some ideas as starting points for developing your own activities. At the end of each activity, the elements of ICT capability that the activities will develop are highlighted. You will need to decide how the activity can best be adapted to match the art and design learning objectives that you have.

Drawing a picture of myself

Children could use digital and video cameras to record themselves. Viewing themselves on screen or a printout gives opportunities for careful observation and subsequent development of the images. As a class, discuss the general features of the images and the sizes, number and colour of features on faces in general. Then introduce children to a paint package and show them how to draw straight and curved lines using the mouse and how to select colours and perhaps the size of the brush itself. Then ask them to draw a picture of themselves using the package. Get the children to focus on a few features of their face, particularly eye and hair style and colour. Depending on the availability of ICT resources this can be done over a short or much longer period of time. The pictures they produce can be turned into a game – match the photograph with the computer drawing – or can be used as a display with the picture and photograph being mounted together. This activity further develops mouse control in terms of movement and in clicking the mouse button. Children should also be taught how to use the print command to print their pictures on to paper. A colour printer is highly desirable for this type of work.

> ## ICT teaching points
>
> ■ Taking digital photographs.
>
> ■ Manipulating images using a paint package.

Draw a picture of a meal

This could be part of a food topic. Using a paint package, each child can draw a picture of a plate containing his or her favourite food and then type in his or her name. Provide them with a large circle for a plate as the starting point. Print out each meal as it is produced. When each child has completed the activity, use the pictures to create a game for the children to guess what each meal consists of. All the pictures from the class could be put into a class PowerPoint presentation, which could then be viewed on either the school's intranet or the website.

> ## ICT teaching points
>
> ■ Basic mouse and features control.
>
> ■ Use of the *brush* tool in a paint package.
>
> ■ Printing out work and comparing the paper and screen versions.

Work of artists

Choose an artist and have a wide selection of his or her paintings available in the form of posters, postcards and books. Discuss with the children the main characteristics of the artist's work – the use of colour, the texture of the work, the way in which people are painted and the content of the pictures themselves. Children could use the Internet to collect information about the artist from a wide range of sources. When you have created a list of the important features, ask the children to produce a painting of their own using a paint program that has similar characteristics. With this age group, this activity will obviously be done at a very simplistic level, but it will allow children to identify particular features of artists' work. This will allow them to make full use of the tools that are available in paint programs including *brush* tools of various widths and *spray can* tools.

> ## ICT teaching points
>
> ■ Allows children to make full use of the tools that are available on paint programs, including *brush* tools of various widths and *spray can* tools.
>
> ■ This activity gives an opportunity to develop children's ability to research in a focused way on the Internet.

Taking a line for a walk

Ask the children to draw a continuous line all over the screen using the *pencil* tool in a paint package. This means that they will create lots of enclosed shapes on the screen. Then ask them to colour in the shapes using the *fill* tool. The challenge is to make sure that no two adjacent shapes have the same colour. This activity will give children an opportunity to practise using some of the basic techniques of a paint package, particularly exploring the range of colours they have available.

ICT teaching points

- Selecting colours.

- Use of *fill* and *pencil* tools.

Investigating the features of a paint package

Children should produce a piece of artwork relevant to their current area of work using traditional artists' media. Scan this into the computer, and then let the children investigate what the features available on the paint package can do. They should save the image under one name, and after each process, they should save the image again under another name. When they have explored the range of effects available, they should print each one out and produce their own display. This will provide a useful reference when they wish to make particular effects in the future.

ICT teaching points

- Scanning images into the computer.

- Using 'save' and 'save as' to keep a record of progress.

- Investigation of the more sophisticated features of a paint package.

- Printing out colour images independently.

Design and produce a decorative logo

This activity can link with many activities, particularly related to designing and making a product in design and technology or creating an identity for a team of children engaged in a group activity. It requires children to make use of a simple draw package and incorporate some text as well. It also provides a good opportunity to talk about suitable font designs and discuss things such as readability versus unusualness. Children may incorporate some clip art element in their design, but they should also be encouraged to manipulate it so that it matches their requirements exactly rather than using as it is. Children can be reminded of the relatively small number of common clip art images which are seen in lots of advertising and handouts.

ICT teaching points

- An understanding of the features of fonts.

- Basic draw skills.

- Importing clip art images.

- Editing clip art images.

- Grouping images together to form the finished logo.

Producing a wallpaper design

The main feature of a wallpaper design is that it is repeated. This activity is ideal to give children the opportunity to use a paint package to create a relatively simple design and then to use copy, cut and paste to produce a wallpaper design using repeating patterns. Children who are familiar and competent with these commands can then be introduced to *rotate* and *mirror* in order to create more sophisticated designs. Draw packages could also be used for this activity, but they would probably need to be designs of a more symmetrical nature. Simple draw packages are fine for straight lines, rectangles and ovals, but other shapes are far more difficult to manipulate.

ICT teaching points

- Basic drawing or painting skills used in a context.

- Using copy, cut and paste.

- Introduction to *rotate*, *mirror* and other more sophisticated tools.

Using artwork in multimedia presentations

There are many opportunities to use children's artwork in multimedia presentations. It can be produced in a range of media, and then scanned in to provide illustrative material. Increasingly children are able to make use of programs such as PowerPoint to communicate their ideas. A useful technique to simulate zooming in on a person is to scan in the same image three times, but zoom in a little each time so that the image of the person takes up more of the screen each time. When the three images are shown one after another you will have created the illusion of simple movement.

ICT teaching points

■ Requires a great deal of time and independent work if the children are to produce a package by themselves.

How can ICT be used specifically in design and technology work?

Entitlement to ICT in Primary Design and Technology (BECTa 2003e) states that ICT can help children's learning in design and technology:

■ by enhancing their capability to explore and develop their ideas;

■ by enhancing their capability to communicate and present their ideas;

■ by providing a range of information sources to enhance their design and technology knowledge;

■ by providing an increased range of tools, equipment, materials and components for their products;

■ by contributing to pupils' awareness of the impact of ICT on the changing world.

Some embryonic activities follow, which focus, in the main, on these particular areas. They should give you some ideas as starting points for developing your own activities. At the end of each activity, the elements of ICT capability that the activities will develop are highlighted. You will need to decide how the activity can best be adapted to match the design and technology learning objectives that you have.

Planning a party

This activity can involve children in planning a simple class party or even something a little bigger. As a group, get the children to think of all the things that they may want at a party. They should then do some research to find out the costs of all the items: food, drinks, entertainer, paper cups and plates etc. In groups they should begin to produce a spreadsheet with 'Items', 'Quantity', 'Cost' and 'Total' as the four headings.

In the total column put a formula that will multiply the quantity (column B, row 2) by the cost (column C, row 2) to give you a total cost for all the paper plates. You can then get the children to copy the formula in column D, row 2 into all the remaining rows in column D. This will then multiply all the costs by the quantity of each item required. At the bottom of column D put a formula to add up the whole row. This will be the total cost of the party. Divide this by the number of people going to the party, and this will give you how much everyone will need to pay. When the children decide that they cannot afford that much, they can start changing

Items	Quantity	Individual Cost	Total	
Paper plates	24	£0.12	=(B2)*(C2)	
Orange squash	2	£0.56		
Sausages	24	£0.22		

FIGURE 8.1 A spreadsheet showing planning for a class party

the figures in the spreadsheet to see where they could save money. 'What if we only had one sausage each, rather than two?', 'What would happen if we bought things from a cheaper shop?' and 'How much money would we save if we did not have a proper disco, but did it ourselves?' are some of the questions the children could investigate.

ICT teaching points

- A simple modelling activity using a spreadsheet.

- Concentrate on 'What happens if I . . . ?' type questions.

Recipe card

Use a desktop publishing package to produce a recipe card for each child's favourite meal. Give the children a basic format of title, photograph or drawing of the finished recipe, ingredients and method, which needs to be printed out on an A5 card. Depending on the previous experience of the children, you can either provide them with a basic template into which they input the information or leave them free to lay out the material as they wish. Ideally, this will be a part of a design and technology activity, where they are actually designing and making a product. Photographs can then be taken, scanned in and incorporated on the recipe card. Care will need to be taken over the way in which the method is written so that it can be easily followed by the intended audience for the recipe cards.

ICT teaching points

- Use of a digital camera and importing a photograph.

- Integration of graphics and text.

- Without the template this is a much more challenging activity.

Making a T-shirt

Ask the children to produce a picture, using a paint package, that illustrates something in which they are interested. They should incorporate their name somewhere on the design. Print this on special paper using an ordinary black and white or colour ink-jet printer. The design can then be ironed on to a plain T-shirt (the children can watch, but this part must be done by adults). This provides very good motivation for them to develop their computer drawing skills and, if you use new T-shirts and sell them to the children, it is a good fund-raiser for the school. If you know that parents can't afford to buy new T-shirts, ask if the children can bring a T-shirt from home to be decorated.

ICT teaching points

- Paint or draw packages could be used, perhaps giving children an opportunity to select which they want to use and why.

- Provides an opportunity to discuss how printers can be used to produce transfers.

Making a noughts and crosses game

Children are asked to make a simple game that could be printed on the back of a cereal packet. As an example you could suggest 'noughts and crosses', for which you will need to produce a playing grid and some small cards with 'O' and 'X' (five of each). Encourage the children to make the pieces as interesting and individual as possible. A draw package would probably be the most suitable for this activity, although a primary-focused computer-aided design package could be introduced at this stage.

ICT teaching points

- Using many features of a draw package.

- A draw package is preferred as it is easier to edit and move elements around.

Designing a house

It is a very time-consuming process to use a drawing package to draw accurately the plan of a house that children may then build. However, there are a number of framework programs that have the components of a house already drawn, and they just have to be included in the appropriate place. A typical example is a 'Tudor house design'. The outcome would be a completed plan of a house, which can be printed on to card and then constructed. The disadvantage of such an approach is that you are very much limited to the designs and sizes that the package provides. There are no opportunities to edit the components. However, it does provide a basic structure and a good foundation on which to base further open-ended work using a proper drawing package.

ICT teaching points

- Selecting and moving images around a screen using a mouse.

- Limited control of size and orientation of elements.

Using a turtle graphics type program to control external traffic lights

Children should extend their use of LOGO from drawing to controlling external events. A simple traffic light set-up using three LEDs connected to the output of a control box can be controlled. (Output A ON; WAIT 3 seconds; Output A OFF; Output B ON; WAIT 3 seconds etc.) Once they have written a program for a single set of traffic lights they could combine it with a second set that would control the traffic in the other direction across the crossroads. This activity could be developed still further so that the traffic on the model road produces an input to the control box that starts the traffic light sequence off (Ager 1997). Children should be encouraged to produce flow diagrams to provide a model of the system.

ICT teaching points

- Build upon their existing work with floor robots and screen turtles.

- If everything is already connected up, it is a relatively straightforward programming activity.

- If children are expected to put the whole thing together, this is a complex ICT activity.

Advertising sign

Building upon their existing work in control, they could devise an advertising sign that incorporates flashing lights and motors. It would be most useful if the advertising was for a school event, and the signs could therefore be used in the reception area of the school to inform all visitors. By incorporating a pressure sensor into the system, the display could be set to start as soon as someone approached the area. Here you are introducing to children the idea of feedback – the sign only works when someone is present. Children may also be able to use simulation programs such as Crocodile Clips to assist in their development of simple circuit design.

ICT teaching points

- Do not let complicated wiring get in the way of simple control principles.

- Simulation programs can be used to speed up the design process.

- Feedback is a relatively complex concept suitable for the top of Key Stage 2.

Designing in three dimensions

There are three-dimensional computer-aided design packages that are affordable and can be used by primary-aged children. They not only allow three-dimensional views but can also provide cardboard nets, with tabs automatically included so that the nets can be cut out and stuck together to form a real three-dimensional model of the representation on screen. Children would be well advised to work on fairly simple three-dimensional shapes or the models will become very difficult to make.

ICT teaching points

- Link the program to previous work with draw packages.

- This is the principle of computer-aided design and manufacture.

How can ICT be used specifically in geography work?

Entitlement to ICT in Primary Geography (BECTa 2003f) identifies five ways in which ICT can enhance children's learning in geography. These are by:

- enhancing their skills of geographical enquiry;
- providing the range of information sources to enhance their geographical knowledge;
- supporting the development of their understanding of geographical patterns and relationships;
- providing access to images of people, places and environments;
- contributing to pupil's awareness of the impact of ICT on the changing world.

Some embryonic activities follow, which focus, in the main, on these particular areas. They should give you some ideas as starting points for developing your own activities. At the end of each activity, the elements of ICT capability that the activities will develop are highlighted. You will need to decide how the activity can best be adapted to match the geography learning objectives that you have.

Map skills with overlay keyboard

Very many simple activities can be linked to the use of an overlay keyboard. A map can be drawn on to the overlay, and particular locations selected, simply by pressing in the correct location. You would also be able to get children to move around the map using the up, down, left and right keys, which could be labelled North, South, West and East.

ICT teaching points

■ Introductory activity with an overlay keyboard.

Visit to a supermarket

When you take the children on a visit to a local supermarket as part of a shopping topic, spend some time looking at the bar codes on each product. Try to arrange beforehand to use an empty till so that you can show them how the bar code is read to tell the computer what the product is, and how much it is, and how this information appears on the till receipt. If you can't arrange this, they can watch the checkout procedure and examine a till receipt. Some supermarkets let customers scan in their own shopping, and with these systems it is easier to arrange for children to get first-hand experience. Here you are emphasising that ICT is used extensively in the outside world, and that computers come in all different shapes and sizes.

ICT teaching points

■ The effect that ICT has on everyday life.

Dressing teddy

Get the children to use a framework program that allows them to fix already prepared images on to an existing background (it can best be thought of as an electronic fuzzy felt). It is a program that can be used right through the age range, but the individual packages are designed for specific age groups. You are provided with an unclothed teddy bear and with a wide range of clothes with which to dress him. Ask children to dress teddy for a hot summer's day, and then for a snowy day in winter. Get the children to produce printouts of each picture for display on the wall. For a long-term project, get pairs of children to dress teddy in an appropriate way for each day's weather. Display the pictures to provide a record of weather over a period of a month.

Later you can do a similar type of activity using a weather map package with symbols as used on television forecasts. This allows text to be included so children could produce their own weather map, including a summary forecast.

ICT teaching points

- Selecting and moving images using a mouse.

- Basic introduction to desktop publishing.

Communication with other people via e-mail/Internet

Increasing use of e-mail and the Internet makes it possible for children to communicate with children and adults in other parts of the country, or world, that they may be studying. This needs to be properly prepared, and should not just be left to chance. It is also possible to search for information on the country's or city's website.

ICT teaching points

- Introduction to basic e-mail.

- Development of more sophisticated Internet searching skills.

Finding out about rivers

Give the children a list of rivers in the world and ask them particular questions about them, such as how long they are, in which country they are and which towns and cities have grown up on their banks. The children should put the answers into a table. They can either be given a basic table template by you, and fill it in, or produce their own table within a word-processing package. In searching for specific information, the task is more focused than merely asking the children to find out about rivers. If you have a range of books and encyclopaedias available, you could get another group doing the same activity with print-based resources and evaluate which method is the most effective.

This activity could be extended to look at local streams and rivers. Using data-logging equipment children could measure temperatures at different positions in the stream. Safety would be of paramount importance in this activity.

ICT teaching points

- Basic table layout in a word processor.

- Simple search techniques.

- Comparison of ICT with non-ICT solution.

- Use of data-logging equipment.

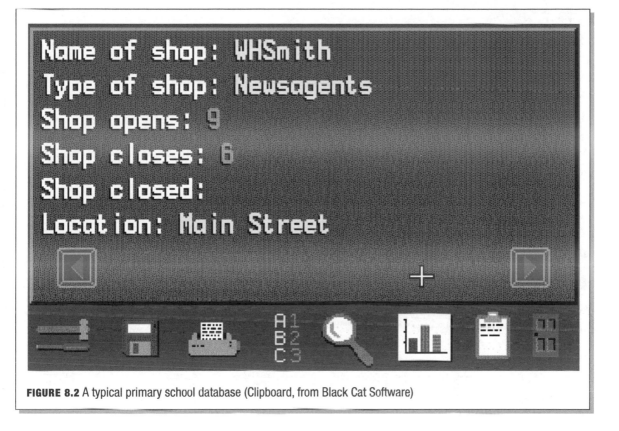

FIGURE 8.2 A typical primary school database (Clipboard, from Black Cat Software)

Shops in the local area

Discuss with the children the shops that are in the local area. Talk about what needs to be known about the shops, i.e. their name, what they sell, opening hours, days on which they are closed, location and so on. As a group talk about the fieldnames and the nature of the data that will be included in the database. This is particularly important in the 'what they sell' field. If children just put in this field a list of items on sale in the shop, then it will make the structure of the database very unwieldy and it will be very difficult to analyse. A single word, such as 'newsagent' or 'butcher', will make the database much more useful. Children should be encouraged to think of questions that the database would help to answer. Easy questions such as 'Which shops open at nine o'clock?' and 'How many newsagents are there in the area?' can be followed by more complex ones, such as 'Which shops stay open the longest?' and 'Is there a link between the shop's location and whether it stays open on Sundays?'

ICT teaching points

- Entering data into an existing database.

- Simple analysis of data.

Holidays in Greece

Discuss with the children the sort of information that is required when you book a holiday. This will enable you to come up with the fieldnames for this holiday database. It is probably more manageable to concentrate on one country and to use old holiday brochures to identify the resorts, the apartments, the hotels, the amenities and the costs. In this activity the children should have some freedom to design the structure of the database themselves. You can then ask each group to answer a series of questions, such as 'Which apartment with swimming pool would be cheapest for a family of four, and what would be its disadvantages?' or 'Which hotel would you recommend for a quiet holiday that did not require too much walking?'

ICT teaching points

■ Design a database.

■ Interrogate the database to answer questions.

■ Analyse graphical representations.

How can ICT be used specifically in history work?

Entitlement to ICT in Primary History (BECTa 2003g) identifies that ICT can help children's learning in history in five ways:

■ it can give them a wider access to the information about some of the characteristic features of the period they are investigating;

■ it can provide a range of sources on disk, CD-ROM or the Internet, which can encourage children to speculate on the results of their investigations, so introducing the idea that the past is represented and interpreted in different ways;

■ it can encourage children to ask questions and discover answers, and then ask more questions when, for example, investigating census data in a database or spreadsheet;

■ it can give them opportunities to select and organise historical information, from a CD-ROM or a website;

■ it can allow them to demonstrate their achievements in communicating their knowledge and understanding of history in a variety of ways, through a graphics package, a word processor or presentational software.

Some embryonic activities follow, which focus, in the main, on these particular areas. They should give you some ideas as starting points for developing your own activities. At the end of each activity, the elements of ICT capability that the activities will develop are highlighted. You will need to decide how the activity can best be adapted to match the history learning objectives that you have.

Use of frameworks to assist in writing

It is often useful to provide children with a structure for continuous prose writing, but a basic question and answer approach can be inflexible. Provide a word processor template that asks a series of questions, providing space for the children to type in their answers. When they have completed their work tell them to delete the questions and then redraft the work so that it reads properly. This strategy can be used to produce a great deal of differentiated work, by giving some children a whole range of very specific questions and others fewer and much broader ones.

ICT teaching points

- Basic word processing.

- Deletion of appropriate text.

- Drafting and redrafting of text.

A Tudor timeline

Provide the children with a desktop publishing file that includes a basic timeline for the Tudor period (1455–1610), with some particular dates marked. They should add events neatly to the timeline and illustrate them with small pieces of appropriate clip art. This will give children practice at moving both images and text around a page to produce a well designed and interesting timeline. Alternatively, groups of children could work on part of the timeline, the individual contributions being combined at the end.

ICT teaching points

- Moving objects around on a page using 'click and drag'.

- Importing graphics.

Graphical representations of events

Using desktop publishing techniques you can produce a flow chart representing particular historical events. It could be as simple as a series of rectangles, their sizes representing for how long a number of kings and queens reigned during a period of history. Alternatively, a historical event could be depicted in the centre of the page, and other rectangles could explain the incidents leading up to the event. This is an alternative strategy to using a narrative account, and it would be possible to enhance the finished product with clip art and drawings. Alternatively, this activity could be done with a database program that allows for the automatic creation of graphs and charts.

ICT teaching points

- Creation of rectangles and other shapes.

- Linking shapes with lines.

- Moving objects around on a page using 'click and drag'.

- Importing graphics.

- Learning how to use a database program.

A Viking diary

It is increasingly likely that children will be able to make use of information from the Internet for some of their work. In this activity children can produce a word-processed diary writing about their life as a Viking. This gives them the opportunity to write in the first person, but to make use of information, not only from books, but from some interesting websites they could access. There are a number of high-quality Viking websites currently available.

ICT teaching points

- Basic word-processing skills.

- Copying from the Internet to a word processor.

- Editing, drafting and redrafting.

Exploring a database

There are many commercially available databases that can be usefully interrogated to get a feel for life in a particular period of history. To get the most out of such an activity children must be familiar with basic search techniques. Working with such a database can be a very sophisticated activity, as some information may not be specifically given, but might be implied. For example, census data for a family might show a father, mother and five children of various ages. Ten years later, the same family might consist of a father, mother and four children. Careful analysis of their ages may enable you to suggest how many of the children died, and how many might have moved to the near-by town. It is important that children realise that they do not actually know what happened, but they can make an intelligent guess.

ICT teaching points

- Search techniques to interrogate a database.

- You may not know all the answers, but what can be inferred?

Victorian style newspaper

Children should be able to manipulate text and pictures by now, so a newspaper project will give them many opportunities to give more detailed consideration to layout (number of columns, size of headlines, placing of graphics etc.), as well as thinking about the audience for their publication. The paper could go on sale around the school as part of a Victorian project day. Small groups of children can be responsible for each page, although there should be some coordination between the groups to ensure a range of stories. They will need to think about appropriate font styles for the Victorian era and will also need to find illustrations (from resource packs or even elderly relatives) that can be scanned into their publication. There are some clip art collections that will have appropriate images.

ICT teaching points

- Scanning images.

- Importing clip art.

- Desktop publishing layout skills

- Drafting and redrafting in a word processor prior to importing into desktop publishing software.

How do you know?

This activity will let children see that some things are easier to find from a CD-ROM based encyclopaedia than others. Give the children a series of facts, and ask them to check whether they are true or false. They should also be able to explain exactly how they found out about the information. 'The Great Pyramid of Khufu is the only one of the Seven Wonders of the Ancient World that is still standing' and 'Victoria was only 18 when she became Queen in 1837' can both be confirmed by simple searches with key words. 'The Wright Brothers flew in the world's first aeroplane before Ford produced the Model T Ford motor car – the world's first mass-produced car', however, requires details from two searches to be analysed. They should also be aware that it is impossible to find out if some statements are true because either the information is not readily available or it was never recorded.

Producing your own encyclopaedia entry

Let children look at the features of a typical CD-ROM encyclopaedia entry and come to a group decision about their characteristics, such as the article name, the nature of the article text (style, reading age etc.), the nature of highlighted text (which leads on to additional articles) and the illustrations. Having discussed the importance of all these features, children should each write their own encyclopaedia entry for an element of the current topic. This could simply be done as a piece of word processing or it could be incorporated into a class's own multimedia encyclopaedia using a multimedia authoring package. It would also be possible to include this information on a school's website, which would make it accessible to the whole world via the Internet.

ICT teaching points

■ Simple word-processing skills.

■ Integration of text and graphics in a multimedia package or on a website.

How can ICT be used specifically in music work?

Entitlement to ICT in Primary Music (BECTa 2003h) identifies ways in which ICT can help children's learning in music. There are four general contexts for implementing music ICT:

■ using and investigating sounds and structures;
■ refining and enhancing performances and compositions;
■ extending knowledge and awareness of styles and conventions;
■ giving wider access to musical experiences.

Some embryonic activities follow, which focus, in the main, on these particular areas. It is perhaps in the music area that the emphasis of ICT encompasses a much wider range of equipment than in other areas. The activities should give you some ideas as starting points for developing your own activities. At the end of each activity, the elements of ICT capability that the activities will develop are highlighted. You will need to decide how the activity can best be adapted to match the music learning objectives that you have.

Drawing music

Use a music package that allows individual sounds to be assigned to icons. Initially, children can reorder the existing icons to create different musical sequences. Subsequently, they can create their own sounds and link them to their own icons.

ICT teaching points

■ Drafting and redrafting information.

Creating musical effects

Read the children a story with a large number of characters in it. Ask each pair of children to choose a sound that they think matches their character. This gives the children an opportunity to explore the range of sounds that are provided with the particular music package. As extension work they could attempt to create the same sound using traditional instruments, their voices or everyday objects.

ICT teaching points

■ Select different sounds from the music package.

Different musical tastes

Create a database for the different kinds of popular music. The categories should be identified by the class as a whole and then the database structure can be devised. This could be done by individual groups of children, which will mean that each group will make their own individual database that will be different from every other group's, or individuals could input data into one class database. Depending on the extent of the database this can be a very simple or much more sophisticated activity.

ICT teaching points

■ Are you inputting data to an existing database or devising your own? The latter requires a much higher level of skill.

Improving their own performance

Karaoke machines are now relatively cheap, and fairly straightforward to use. In this activity, the focus would be on getting the child to improve his or her own performance after singing along to a particular track and receiving feedback. The ICT element is involved in setting up the karaoke machine and the tape recorder that will be used to record their performances.

ICT teaching points

- Competent use of microphones, minidisc, tape recording and karaoke equipment.

Adding percussion

Provide the children with a melody on a computer-based music program. They can hear the music play, and see it on the screen as a form of musical notation. They then experiment with the music by adding percussion to the melody. They are able to change their ideas as often as they want until they are happy with their contribution.

ICT teaching points

- Drafting and redrafting their ideas.

- Relating the musical notation to characteristics of the sound.

Exploring musical styles

Play children a piece of music representative of a particular musical style. Discuss its main features. Then ask children to discover more about the style by interrogating a CD-ROM that contains the sounds of many musical instruments, both individually and in ensemble. Here children need to develop searching strategies slightly different from those they may be used to, as they are looking for sounds rather than words. They should, however, be encouraged to use some strategy rather than just trial and error.

ICT teaching points

- Developing a search strategy for interrogating a database focusing on sounds.

Guitar tutor

There are now a number of computer-based learning packages that teach children how to play the guitar (and other instruments as well). They really make the most of the multimedia environment, with video showing the position of both hands on the guitar, animations of the chord fingering and the sound of the whole piece of music or just individual chords. This is probably most useful outside the classroom environment, and will give clear structure to practice sessions at home.

ICT teaching points

- Children need to be able to navigate around the package, by clicking the mouse pointer on buttons.

- In this application the computer is being used to enhance learning.

- No ICT skills are being developed.

How can ICT be used specifically in physical education?

The use of ICT in PE at Key Stages 3 and 4 became compulsory in September 2000, but this is not the case with Key Stages 1 and 2. However, there are significant contributions that ICT can make to the teaching of PE in the primary school.

Some embryonic activities follow, which focus, in the main, on these particular areas. They should give you some ideas as starting points for developing your own activities. At the end of each activity, the elements of ICT capability that the activities will develop are highlighted. You will need to decide how the activity can best be adapted to match the PE learning objectives that you have.

Team tactics

By using large display technology and software such as PowerPoint it is possible to build up diagrams of sports pitches that can be used to discuss tactics. Simple animations can be built into each presentation, showing the most effective movement of players in particular situations. This can be used as a teaching resource, or children can contribute to the resource.

ICT teaching points

- Children can develop their ICT capability with presentation programs.

- The presentation, once prepared, can be used many times over.

Sports data

Data collection and analysis fits in well with much work in physical education. By collecting data such as sex, height, weight, reach, leg length, best high jump, best long jump and best obstacle race time, children would be able to look for patterns in the data using a database. There are also plenty of opportunities for sorting data in different categories.

You can record children's performances over a period of time in a range of athletic events, and see if all children improve at the same rate. Analysis could develop much further to identify the type of body characteristics that seem to be needed for long distance running and sprints, for example. More extensive work could compare the class's results with national averages. This work would be most appropriately done using a spreadsheet.

ICT teaching points

- Data can be used to identify current performance and to set targets for improvement.

Technique analysis

With relatively cheap digital video recorders and notebook computers it is feasible to record individual children's sporting technique, and they are able to watch it while on the sports field to identify ways in which they can improve. Software is also available that will allow the video to be slowed down and analysed.

ICT teaching points

- Immediate feedback to sporting performance can be given.

How can ICT be used specifically in religious education?

Entitlement to ICT in Religious Education (BECTa 2003i) identifies the ways in which ICT has the potential to help children by:

- enhancing their investigative skills in RE;
- assessing and using critically a wide range of information;
- organising, recording, reporting and communicating findings.

Some embryonic activities follow, which focus, in the main, on these particular areas. They should give you some ideas as starting points for developing your own activities. At the end of each activity, the elements of ICT capability that the activities will develop are highlighted. Many of the activities described in the history section would also be appropriate for religious education. You will need to decide how the activity can best be adapted to match the religious education learning objectives that you have.

A database of religions

A database could be set up to identify common features across different cultures and religions. A clear structure would need to be provided, with children being aware of the terms 'field' and 'record'. A whole series of questions could then be asked to find commonalities and differences between religions. For these questions to be answered appropriately a great deal of care needs to go into the design of the database.

ICT teaching points

- Using a database is relatively easy and is likely to match RE learning outcomes.

- Producing your own database is more complex but will develop more ICT capability.

Presentation on religion

Children could produce a PowerPoint presentation covering the basic features of one religion. This could be done in groups, so that the rest of the class could learn about the other religions by using the presentations. Alternatively, the whole class could be involved in producing one multimedia package, which could then be used as a resource for other classes in the school. There are a number of content-rich CD-ROMs that cover aspects of religion and faith, which could be useful sources of information. Further resources could be sought from the Internet, but you need to select the sites beforehand, as there is much inappropriate material that might be seen if children do free searches using words such as 'Religion', 'Christian', 'Muslim' or 'Jewish'.

ICT teaching points

- The production of a presentation that will be used by a real audience is a motivating activity.

- Children will probably have the ICT capability to undertake the task, so that the learning can focus on the RE issues.

CHAPTER

9

ICT and the Foundation Stage

How can ICT support the six areas of learning of the Foundation Stage?

The Foundation Stage curriculum consists of six areas of learning, with each area being broken down into Early Learning Goals. The publication *Curriculum Guidance for the Foundation Stage* (QCA 2000) provides example material illustrating aspects of children's learning that should be evident when they enter compulsory education. This document also provides details of Stepping Stones along the way, which show the way in which children can meet the Early Learning Goals in a progressive way.

ICT is specifically identified in the 'Knowledge and understanding of the world' section of the curriculum. The Early Learning Goal for this section is broken down into the following Stepping Stones, showing progression from the age of three.

Show an interest in ICT

Teachers need to give children the opportunities to control something like a floor robot, help them to become aware of technology around them, such as washing machines, telephones, cash registers and burglar alarms, and stimulate children's interest in using ICT, such as computer activities and interactive whiteboards. Children wanting to play with a programmable toy, using a computer program or role-playing the use of technological equipment would be evidence to show that this Stepping Stone was being achieved.

Know how to operate simple equipment

Teachers need to teach simple skills such as switching things on or off, to give children the opportunity to take things apart to see how they work and to develop the ICT skills children may have acquired at home. Children knowing how and when to operate a pelican crossing under supervision would be evidence of this Stepping Stone being achieved.

Complete a simple program on the computer and/or perform simple functions on ICT apparatus

Teachers need to encourage children to use things like a tape recorder and headphones, a programmable toy and a mouse to click on icons to cause things to happen in a computer program. Children also need the opportunity to role-play the use of ICT and to be introduced to appropriate technical language such as 'eject' and 'double click'. Independent rewinding of a cassette tape when the music has finished would be evidence that this Stepping Stone had been achieved.

The Stepping Stones lead to the Early Learning Goal of 'Find out about and identify the uses of everyday technology and use information and communications technology and programmable toys to support their learning'.

Teachers need to give children the opportunity to explore the use of ICT across all their learning. This may include the use of a talking word processor to develop language and communication, talking books for early reading, a paint program for mark making, a telephone for speaking and listening and CD-ROMs, video and audio tapes for finding things out. Children should also be able to talk, and share their knowledge about, ICT that they see within their own environment, such as traffic lights outside the school and bar code scanners in supermarkets. If you were to see children in role-play situations typing letters and printing them out you would have evidence to show that this Early Learning Goal was being achieved.

However, it is clear that the effective use of ICT can also enhance almost all of the work in the Foundation Stage and the following sections detail how ICT can support work in these six areas of learning.

Personal, social and emotional development

Much of the work that children will do on computers will be as one of a pair. Strategies need to be devised to encourage cooperation and learning to share both ideas and time using the mouse or keyboard. Even at this age children should be encouraged to become independent in their use of the computer, developing skills of independent learning and decision-making. Children working in a group on a computer-based activity can be stimulated to discuss their work and many of these activities will ensure that children remain interested, excited and motivated by the work.

Communication, language and literacy

Here children will benefit greatly from the multimedia machines and applications that are available to them. The way in which pictures, words and sounds can easily be coordinated provides a very rich experience for young children. Talking story books that highlight the words as they are spoken and include animation encourage children to interact with the machine. The animation, sounds and pictures encourage the children to interpret what they see and to be better able to understand the meaning. Talking word processors provide a very real link between the children's ideas, the words they speak, what the words look like and what they sound like. At this age the teacher or adult helper may need to type in the children's ideas, but the clear link between a word on the screen, the sound that the word makes and the child being responsible for choosing that particular word is clearly very motivating.

There are a wide range of interactive websites available, many of which are free, but the subscription sites can be purchased using e-learning credits, details of which can be found on the Curriculum Online website (www.curriculumonline.gov.uk). As children are introduced to floor robots considerable amounts of discussion, cooperation and problem-solving need to go on between children in order to get the robot to move as desired.

There are many programs that encourage letter recognition, which show in an animated way how the letter is formed and which provide the sounds they make as well. Multimedia authoring applications could also be used to develop children's oral language skills. Using a digital camera, photographs could be taken of children after a day visit to the zoo. Each child could have his or her picture taken with an animal in the background. Back at school, each child could have his or her voice recorded saying something about a favourite animal. This could all be linked together as a PowerPoint presentation, for the children themselves to use, and also as a way for the parents of the children to see what progress they are making.

For the vast majority of these activities the basic ICT skills that will be developed involve use of overlay and ordinary keyboards and mouse control. Most of the time that will be spent on these activities is related to language and number work and not ICT.

Children are often more willing to experiment with their ideas on a computer screen, rather than on a piece of paper. They can get confused by the general use of upper case letters on keyboards when they want to use lower case, but you can buy stickers to go on the keys, or lower case keyboards are available. Alternatively, you can have a cardboard copy of a keyboard near the computer so that children can refer to if they have a problem.

Mathematical development

All aspects of numeracy can be explored in a colourful and interactive way. In particular there are many programs that can be used for matching, sorting and shape recognition. Increasingly, the use of interactive whiteboards in the classroom will allow young children to interact with this type of program just by touching images and moving them around with their fingers. This type of work should not replace practical activity, but it is a good link between concrete and more abstract mathematical thinking. The power of animation can also usefully be exploited to explore other mathematical concepts, such as bigger than, smaller than, in front of or behind. Again, this should not replace demonstration by the teacher using physical objects, but it can easily consolidate such work. Here again it is likely that the ICT skills that are developed are almost exclusively related to simple mouse operation, where correct responses have to be clicked on. This is relevant and useful skill practice, but even though the child is sitting in front of the computer the amount of ICT being developed is very small. Almost all the emphasis in this type of activity is on numeracy. Children should also work with floor robots to learn about simple control and investigate ideas such as forwards and backwards, giving them the opportunity to use mathematical language to describe position and size. They should increasingly show awareness of number operations, and begin to use the language involved.

Knowledge and understanding of the world

Although it will be difficult for children to draw clear representations using art packages, it is possible for them to lay out scenes using characters available in framework programs. By, for example, adding different furniture to the layout of a room they can become more overtly familiar with their everyday environment. The use of CD-ROM titles gives children opportunities to explore different parts of the world or different times in history in an interactive and exciting way. Clearly, however, the titles should be chosen carefully so that children can gain something from them because of their visual and audio content rather than the text, which in most cases is likely to be written at far too high a level. It is probably more effective to use this type of program with the teacher in control, with the material being displayed using a digital projector or an interactive whiteboard. The teacher can then make the biggest impact with the visual and audio elements, but can also talk to the children and ask questions at a level appropriate for the particular group.

Children will already be aware of much of the ICT that is around them, and this should not just include computers, but encompass all aspects of communication, such as television, video recorders, digital cameras, digital video cameras, cable, satellite, telephones, including mobiles and fax machines, microwaves, automated teller machines and bar scanners. Children will also be able to use programmable toys or floor robots, both to understand that inanimate objects can be given instructions that they will follow, and to develop children's spatial awareness and sequencing skills. This links in well with much of the numeracy work they will be doing.

Physical development

This is where the focus on mouse and keyboard skills is so important. Hand–eye coordination and control over small hand movements are vital areas to develop if children are going to be able to use the computers that are currently available in schools. Notice that these in particular are skills that children in previous generations had no need to learn, and it is perhaps worth considering that as input to computers develops to be based more on speech, perhaps in a decade or two's time, these specific ICT skills will no longer need to be developed.

Creative development

Computers allow children to develop a creative interest in music at a very early age. Small keyboards now have the facility to record and replay a series of notes, and computer programs can have particular sounds linked to pictures, so that by reordering the pictures, different sequences of sounds can be produced. Art packages, in addition to, not instead of, more traditional artists' media can be introduced, with children focusing upon the ease of altering the image compared with doing so using more permanent media.

What is the specific ICT capability that children need to develop?

In the early years of primary education children need to develop the basic ICT technical skills that they will use for much of their future schooling and their adult life. They need to become familiar with ICT in its broadest form and positive users of it.

There are probably two basic areas that children need to develop, and these are the techniques that will enable them to interact with the computer. They need to input information into the computer using a range of keyboards, and they also need to be able to use a mouse effectively.

1	2	3	4	5	6	7	8	9	10	11	12	13	14	15
16	17	18	19	20	21	22	23	24	25	26	27	28	29	30
31	32	33	34	35	36	37	38	39	40	41	42	43	44	45
46	47	48	49	50	51	52	53	54	55	56	57	58	59	60
61	62	63	64	65	66	67	68	69	70	71	72	73	74	75
76	77	78	79	80	81	82	83	84	85	86	87	88	89	90
91	92	93	94	95	96	97	98	99	100	101	102	103	104	105

FIGURE 9.1 A basic overlay keyboard

1	2	3	4	5	6	7	8	9	10	11	12	13	14	15
16	17	18	19	20	21	22	23	24	25	26	27	28	29	30
31	32	33	34	35	36	37	38	39	40	41	42	43	44	45
46	47	48	49	50	51	52	53	54	55	56	57	58	59	60
61	62	63	64	65	66	67	68	69	70	71	72	73	74	75
76	77	78	79	80	81	82	83	84	85	86	87	88	89	90
91	92	93	94	95	96	97	98	99	100	101	102	103	104	105

FIGURE 9.2 The overlay keyboard divided into nine sections

Keyboard skills

When children are first introduced to computers they will probably input information using an overlay keyboard. The keyboard is like a pressure sensitive mat, and is usually divided up into 255 small squares, each of which operates as a press switch.

The overlay keyboard is used with software that allows you to link pressing a particular spot on the keyboard to a particular action occurring on the screen. In early use the squares are often linked together to form much larger rectangles. This makes it easy for young children to press the appropriate section of the keyboard and to get the appropriate response.

Using the software provided you design your overlay on the computer, first dividing up the A4 or A3 space into large areas, so that there are substantial pads that can be pressed by the young child. Now you will add text and pictures to your overlay, and decide what you will want to happen when the particular section is pressed. At its simplest you will probably want the word to come on to the screen of a word processor. It is also possible for images to appear on screen, for sounds to be heard or for words to be read out.

As in the example shown in Figure 9.3, children are able to write simple sentences into a word-processing program, such as 'This is a cat' and 'This is a spider', by pressing the appropriate areas of the keyboard. In this example, children are only allowed to move to a new line (i.e. the enter key) or to rub out what they have typed (i.e. the backspace key deleting one letter at a time). It would be possible for a picture of a cat, dog or spider to appear on the screen when the appropriate areas were pressed. You could also have the words spoken as they are pressed.

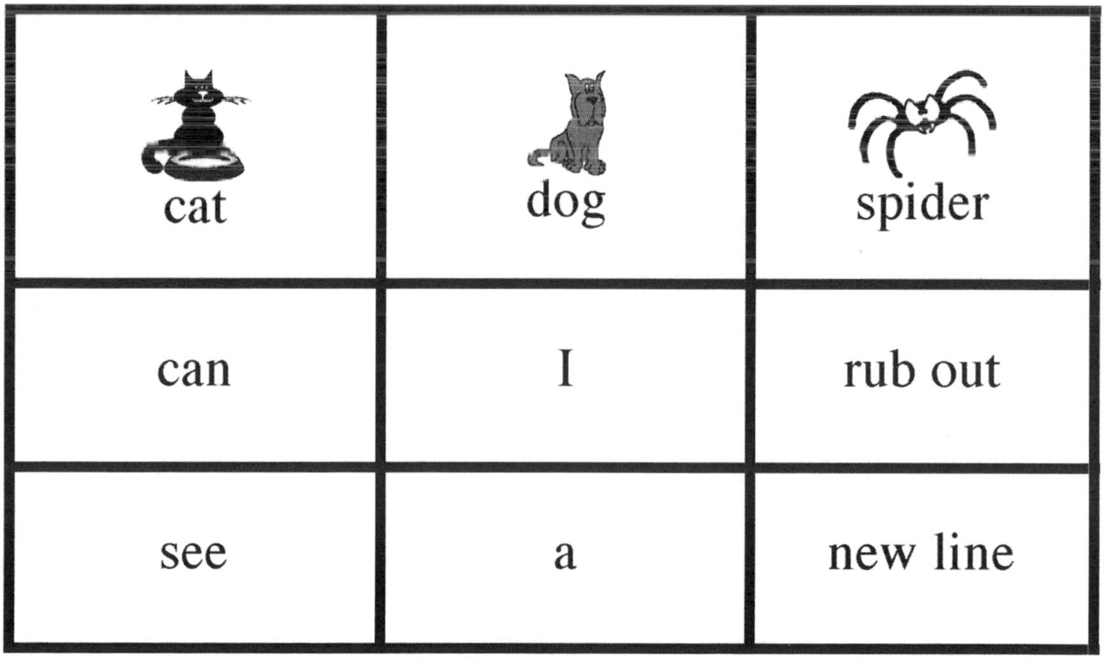

cat	dog	spider
can	I	rub out
see	a	new line

FIGURE 9.3 A very simple overlay that fits over the keyboard

In this example there are severe limitations put on the way in which children use the program. All the words the children need are on the overlay. Further work can make use of overlays that have only some of the words, with a section of the keyboard allowing children to input individual letters and spaces. Later still you can simulate a full keyboard, with the keys being written in lower case, and perhaps being in alphabetical order rather than the traditional 'qwerty' layout. But you do not have to make up your own overlays. They are readily available in a wide range of different contexts from many software suppliers.

At a later stage still you can integrate the use of the overlay keyboard with the computer's existing keyboard. More complicated words are available on the overlay, but simpler words are expected to be typed into the ordinary keyboard. The use of the overlay does not have to be limited to text, but can be effectively used with numbers and for simulation games.

On-screen word lists

As an intermediate strategy between using an overlay keyboard and using the full keyboard, there are programs available that allow prepared lists of words to appear on one edge of the screen when some other application is open. This allows more complicated words to be selected from the list by a mouse click, and they automatically appear in the open application. This does mean that the ordinary keyboard is still available for children to input individual letters for spelling simpler words.

Mouse skills

The mouse is a device that children (and many adults) will take a little time to get used to. Children need to be introduced to programs in which simple mouse control is needed to interact with the material, and talking story books provide an ideal example. These are discussed in more detail in the English section of Chapter 7, but an important element of the programs is the way in which pointing and clicking at many items in the picture cause amusing animation to be seen and sounds to be heard. These programs are very motivating to young children because of the degree of interaction that can take place.

A problem that needs to be considered is the size of the mouse compared with the child's hands. A mouse usually consists of two or three switches mounted around a ball that rolls freely over surfaces such as the material out of which mouse mats are made. The ball in turn moves two small rollers, one of which moves the pointer on the screen up and down, with the other moving it from side to side. When you move the mouse diagonally both rollers move and the pointer moves from one corner of the screen to the other. The software associated with the mouse then takes over and gives you a great many options. The one that is most useful with children of this age is the speed control. As a competent computer user you can move the mouse easily all over the screen. If you slow it down it becomes very frustrating because you have to move the mouse a great distance on the mouse mat to move it a much smaller distance, and relatively slowly, to the place you want. For a young child learning to use the equipment this is what is needed. Some individual programs allow you to change the speed of pointer travel, or it can be done for all programs by altering the mouse section of the computer operating system. Mice are now available that appear to function in the same way, but use light rather than mechanical rollers.

Very early on children also need to be taught to pick up the mouse and reposition it in relation to the computer. In many classrooms you are likely to find children with mice being operated at arm's length, with the child moving further and further away from the computer screen. This is where a mouse mat is useful, as the child can be told always to work with the mouse near the middle of the mouse mat. You will then need to teach children the technique of sliding the mouse and then lifting it up slightly, so that their mouse hand is always at a sensible distance from the computer and the screen.

You may find that some children find using the pointing device called a roller ball much easier. This is like a mouse turned upside down, with the switches moved and the ball itself being made much larger. The device itself remains stationary, and you use your fingers to roll the ball to get the pointer to move. This gets over many of the problems associated with a mouse, but it is probably not as quick to operate, and most children will need to learn how to use a traditional mouse anyway at some stage. It is perhaps best used by those who are having considerable difficulties using a mouse, rather than as a starting point for all children.

As children become used to the operation of the mouse you can gradually increase the speed so that it becomes less time-consuming and frustrating to the children.

The other element of the mouse is its switches. There are generally two or three switches on mice, with the one most commonly used being the left one. Children must be taught that pressing the left button is known as 'left click', and pressing the right hand one is 'right click'. However, at this early stage whenever they are told to 'click' the mouse it should be the left button that is used. For left handed children it is possible to swap over the operations of the left and right handed buttons, so that they can 'click' on the button nearest their forefinger (the right hand one) and still get the operations associated with the left button. In many programs written for young children both buttons operate in exactly the same way. It is only as you begin to use more sophisticated programs, in which the left, right and possibly centre buttons provide you with a wide range of on-screen options, that you need to worry too much about which button the children are pressing.

At this stage children will need to be taught two mouse techniques. The first is 'clicking' on part of a picture to instigate an event, such as animation or sound. The two elements of moving the pointer to the right place on the screen and then 'left clicking' the mouse can initially be carried out as two distinct actions, although, with time, you would hope to see a coordinated action of movement and 'clicking', with the hand staying comfortably over the mouse. Children should not grip the mouse, but hold it quite gently with the palm of their hand resting gently on the body of the mouse, and the forefinger positioned over the main button.

The second technique, which is used extensively in framework programs, involves clicking on a particular image on the screen. The image now appears to stick to the pointer and will move around the screen wherever the pointer goes. The next time you click the mouse button, the image will be stuck once again to the background. This clearly gives a simple way of re-arranging images on a screen – a little like electronic fuzzy felt (see Chapter 5). This is good practice for a similar, but slightly more complicated, technique that is used extensively in all major software applications, called 'click and drag'. In this technique you click on an object to select it, and then, keeping your finger on the left button, you drag the image across the screen until it is in the correct position. Then you release your finger from the left button, and the image stays where it is. This requires children to have considerable dexterity, and should only be introduced to children when they can happily work with the other techniques, and obviously when they start using programs that use 'click and drag'.

A final technique that should be introduced as children become more capable mouse users is 'double click'. Again, this is a technique that is used infrequently in programs designed for very young children, but as soon as they are given an opportunity to load their own choice of programs from a computer they will need to use this technique, as it is the way in which many programs are usually started.

A 'double click' means that you press the mouse button twice in succession, quickly. Again, you can set up from within your computer how large or small the gap between the two presses can be in order to count as a 'double click'. Do not, however, make the gap too large, as what is intended as two 'single clicks' will be interpreted as one 'double click', with totally different consequences. 'Double clicks' are usually used to select and run programs from their program icons on screen, or to select areas of text in word processing applications. Indeed, for some features 'triple clicks' are needed, but we do not need to consider them with children of this age.

Where children have access to an interactive whiteboard they are able to achieve a more natural and immediate interaction with software. By using a special stylus, or with some versions just their finger, they are able to select and move items around a large screen. This not only makes the interaction more intuitive, it also allows for group activities to be undertaken, emphasising cooperation, discussion and decision-making.

Main teaching issues

- Children's activities should encourage them to become enthusiastic and positive users of ICT.

- Basic keyboard and mouse skills are priority ICT issues at this age.

- Make sure you know where the focus of the activity is. Is it ICT or is it something else making use of ICT?

- Take into account previous home use of ICT in a positive way.

Avoid

- Practising ICT skills in isolation.

- Using ICT when a well illustrated book could be just as effective.

10

ICT and Inclusion

What does inclusion mean in education?

Inclusion means increasing the participation of children in the cultures, curriculum and communities of local schools. Inclusion is concerned with supporting the individual learning needs of all children, not just those who are characterised as having special educational needs. ICT is a vital tool for ensuring that inclusion actually happens.

How can ICT help with special educational needs?

This section gives only a very broad overview of the ways in which ICT can be used with children who have special educational needs. In summary, all the power of the computer to motivate, interest and enthuse, through graphics, movement and sound, can be used, in the same way as for children without special educational needs, but in many cases we need to find alternative ways in which the children can interact with the computer. In this chapter the types of hardware and software that are available are identified and teaching approaches suggested. The material here relates to children in mainstream primary education with special educational needs. It does not discuss the issue in the depth required for children in special schools.

What are the main issues to consider for children with physical disabilities?

Children with physical disabilities will want to use the computer for exactly the same range of tasks as children of their own age without physical disabilities. The requirement, therefore, is to assist children in interacting with the computer by the use of specialised input devices.

Keyboards

Keyguards can be fixed over existing keyboards. In their simplest form they consist of a metal sheet with holes in, the holes corresponding to the location of the keys. This means that the child has to make a distinct movement with his or her fingers through each hole to press the appropriate key. If the hand just drags along the keyboard, for example, no key is pressed, as the metal plate prohibits contact. Keyguards are best used in conjunction with alterations to the 'key repeat' settings, which can usually be done through the operating system interface. When you keep your finger on a key for a second or so, that letter starts repeating on the screen. This can be useful, but in this case the option should be turned off so that it does not matter how long a child keeps a finger on a key, as it will just produce one letter.

There are some children who will find it better to use a much smaller keyboard, perhaps because it involves less overall movement. Alternatively, much wider ergonomic keyboards are readily available – these are specially designed to avoid repetitive strain injury, but may be appropriate for some children. There are also much larger keyboards, with larger keys, which make it easier for some children to type, and overlay keyboards, discussed in earlier chapters, which allow greater customisation of the keyboard.

'Sticky keys' is a function available in some operating systems, which gets over the problem of a child being unable to press two keys at once. You would want to do this, for example, when using *shift* followed by a key press to give a single upper case letter at the start of a sentence, or *control* followed by a key press to format some text in a word processor. This can be switched on from within the program, and gives an audible warning to remind children that they are using the feature.

Pointing devices

The traditional mouse as a pointing device is often much too difficult for children with physical disabilities to use. Alternatives are rollerballs, effectively a mouse turned upside down so that the child makes the ball move and the body of the device stays still, and joysticks. With rollerballs the ball itself can be made quite large so that it is easy to manipulate, but again a device like this must be used in conjunction with software that allows other alterations to the way in which the pointer is linked to the rollerball and buttons. The speed of the pointer needs to be controlled carefully so that it is not so slow that it requires extensive input from the child, but not so quick that it is difficult to control precisely.

The most common features of mouse use are probably 'click and drag' and 'double click', both of which require considerable fine motor control. Software can be configured so that the first click selects the item and 'sticks' it to the pointer, and the second click drops it on screen, so that the child does not have to keep a finger on the button and move the rollerball at the same time. It is also possible to make a single button click equivalent to a 'double click' using appropriate software.

Switches

Many children with physical disabilities can only interact with a computer by pressing a switch, or a number of switches. These come in a wide range of configurations, shapes and bright colours, and also with a range of fixings so that they can be fitted on to wheelchairs or furniture at appropriate heights and angles. It should be emphasised that considerable skill is required to use switches properly, in the same way that it takes time for children to learn how to use a mouse, so adequate training must be given before children will feel confident in using them. Software is available that will give switch access to many standard pieces of software, although a number of companies specialise in producing software that is specially designed for use with switches.

The main feature of switch software is the way in which one or two switches can be used to control the main features of a pieces of software. This is done by scanning (this should not be confused with the scanning of photographs into paint packages). Let us take an example of a child having to make a choice from four pictures to match with a word at the top of the screen. In its traditional mode of operation, the mouse would be used to click on the appropriate image, and this would result in a computer response that would vary, depending on whether the selection was right or wrong. If this program operated in scanning mode, the four images at the bottom of the page would be automatically highlighted, one at a time, for a period determined by the software configuration. The child would need to press the switch when the appropriate response was highlighted. There are now switch and scanning programs that can be integrated with talking story books, so that all the places where animations and sounds occur are highlighted and scanned, giving children the opportunity to stop the scanning at any point to see the feature come to life.

This technique can be used in more sophisticated ways with an on-screen letter grid or word bank that can be controlled by the scanning process and switches being linked to a word processor, which takes up the other part of the screen. With a predictive word processor, children are able to select from a list of words that appear on the screen as a result of the child typing in a few letters of a word. Software like this helps to reduce the effort required to input text for children with physical disabilities.

Other forms of input

Sensors can detect a child's movement, and this then allows interaction with the computer. With voice recognition software, which is increasingly available, children speak into a microphone and the words automatically appear in a word-processing package. Software of this type takes up a lot of memory, and it also needs considerable time to 'teach' the software how the child speaks. The software needs to be customised for each child. This is an area in which improvements are being rapidly made.

What are the main issues to consider for children with cognitive and learning difficulties?

Much of the software for use with children with learning difficulties is also used by other children in a similar classroom situation. The likelihood is that some older children with learning difficulties will be using content-rich software similar in nature to that which is normally used by much younger children. It is therefore vital that the work is set in appropriate contexts, suitable for the age of the child. Content-free software will be used by these children for much the same reasons as any other, such as the speed with which errors can be corrected in a word-processing package, the wealth of experiences using a wide range of media that can be experienced when using a good CD-ROM package and the sense of self-esteem that can be engendered when a well presented piece of work, of equivalent standard to everyone else in the class, is produced. Framework programs are particularly important here, since they were initially designed for use by children with special educational needs. The wide range of content covered, while still using the basic techniques of clicking and moving objects around the screen, ensures that there is appropriate material for all age groups.

What are the main issues to consider for children with visual impairment?

The first consideration in supporting children with visual impairment is to ensure that the screen display is as clear as possible. Make sure that no light from nearby windows can cause glare on the screen, and ensure that screen colours are chosen to give a high contrast between text and background. Also check that clear text fonts are used, and that the default size of text is fairly large. In a word processor, this can usually be done by changing the 'Normal' style. Screen magnification software is also available, the most sophisticated of which will easily allow different views to be identified.

Some children may find it useful to have labels on the keys showing the letters as large as possible. You might even consider identifying some of the more important keys, such as Enter, Shift, Ctrl and Alt, with a textured material so that the children can quickly identify the layout of the keyboard.

Once children have access to the facilities of a computer, they will immediately benefit from the advantages. Compare a child's access to a CD-ROM encyclopaedia (any multimedia computer could be used) with that to one written in Braille (the amount of storage space required and cost would be prohibitive for many institutions). Touch screens that are fixed over existing monitors, or increasingly integrated into purpose built ones, allow ease of access for interaction between the child and the information. If the answer appears on the screen, you do not need to find the appropriate key on a keyboard to press – you just press the screen. There is also a great deal of software that can produce very bright patterns, which can be very stimulating. The software can be used by the children as they develop their ICT skills, or can be designed as part of the reward system.

Speech software is now available that allows visually impaired children to talk to the computer. Not only words are understood, but also the commands for navigating from place to place in the program. Similarly, programs that speak letters, words and sentences as they are typed are becoming more common, and will provide children with reliable feedback related to the keyboard input they make.

The scanning technique, making use of a traditional keyboard, overlay keyboard or switches, can be used to great effect with many programs, particularly those that use 'point and click' techniques, such as talking story books.

There are also many ways in which Braille can be integrated into computer use. The computer is able to produce Braille straight from text input to the computer with suitable software and a Braille embosser. Alternatively, text can be scanned into a computer and analysed using optical character recognition software. This can then be read using synthetic speech software.

What are the main issues to consider for children with specific learning difficulties?

Specific learning difficulties relate particularly to writing, perhaps linked to dyslexia, reading and basic mathematical skills. Many of the strategies suggested earlier will be useful here, particularly overlay keyboards with word banks and screen-based word banks integrated with a word processor. An important tool for this group of children is the spell checker, which obviously comes in a number of forms. A small spell checker, similar in size to a calculator, can be a useful aid, and is much easier to use than a traditional dictionary. The problem is, and always has been, that in order to look up how to spell a word, you need to have some idea of how the word is spelt. Using an electronic spell checker you can input your 'best guess' and you are provided with a range of possibilities. The child now knows the correct spelling of a number of words, but does not necessarily know which word is the one he or she wants.

Screen-based spell checkers integrated into word-processing packages are extremely easy to use compared to looking up words in dictionaries. The most sophisticated ones underline words that are incorrectly spelt as you type. When you 'right click' on the underlined words, you are provided with a small window containing the computer's idea of what you were trying to type. You now 'left click' on the correct word, and it is immediately placed in the text. Sometimes it works very well, as when I typed 'imediately' and got only 'immediately', but when I checked 'tipe' I got 'tie', 'type', 'tip', 'tiptoe' and 'tipple'. Ensure that you disable the option to add words to your own custom dictionary. If children do add their own misspelled words, then they will no longer be identified as incorrectly spelt, and as far as the child is concerned, their spelling will have improved considerably – there were no red lines under any words.

A further feature that needs care in its use is AutoCorrect, where a database of common spelling or typing errors, together with the correct versions, is searched as you are typing. As soon as one of the 'errors' is discovered it is automatically changed to the 'correct' word, according to the database. The database is easily customised to include all an individual's spelling quirks. The danger is that children will continually type in the letters in the incorrect order, but the computer will automatically make it right with no intervention. This will not improve the motivation of children to learn to spell correctly.

A talking word processor is also useful, allowing individual letters, words and sentences to be spoken. The feedback that children can get on an individual basis from the computer is useful, in that the child not only sees that the word is spelt wrongly, but can also hear that it does not sound right.

As for all children, if the spelling and mathematical activities can be done in interesting and fun ways, then the children are more likely to be motivated to engage in them. There are many CD-ROM based literacy and numeracy programs that offer a wide range of interactive and educational experiences. One thing to consider, however, is that although the level of the work may need to be simpler than for other children in the class, its context needs to be appropriate for the age and interests of the children concerned. Children will not be motivated by what they view as 'babyish' work.

What are the main issues to consider for children with hearing impairments?

For children with hearing impairments, the visual powers of the computer need to be concentrated upon. Signing programs are available, and within a very short time they will become available as an integrated part of a word-processing package. Programs that create links between words and pictograms are available. Using these, children can add words in a word processor by selecting particular pictures. Children find sounds, however limiting, more meaningful if they can be linked to visual experiences.

The use of video conferencing over the Internet allows children with hearing impairments to communicate by signing with children in other parts of the country or the world. There are also opportunities for children to use exciting, content-rich CD-ROM based multimedia packages, and where appropriate to link the sound output of the computer to their own enhanced amplification system. Children can also make use of multimedia authoring packages, such as PowerPoint, to make their own visually stimulating interactive material in a form to which they can easily relate.

Wherever possible children should be involved in practical activities in which they use their sight. This offers opportunities for using floor robots, analysing the information received from remote sensors or controlling models using some form of programming language.

What are the main issues to consider for children with speech and language difficulties?

These children need to undertake activities that develop their language. Using appropriate input devices they can use software that responds in a visual way if a sentence is produced that is grammatically correct. Children are therefore encouraged to check the syntax of their work carefully. The pictures that are produced as a result of the sentences illustrate what they have been writing about, and when printed out can form the basis for future talking and writing work. By using overlay keyboards, or on-screen word banks, children are able to concentrate on sentence structure, rather than on individual word formation.

Talking word processors are viewed by some as effective in providing feedback to the child by linking a typed word with a particular sound. However, the synthesised speech that is available does not provide a good model for children with these particular difficulties. Increasingly, the quality of the output is improving to provide speech of the standard of talking story books, and is a digital recording of a real human voice rather than a synthesis of individual sounds.

Children can also record their own speech, and incorporate it into multimedia authoring programs, allowing them to increase their self-esteem, as their own voice becomes part of a computer package.

What are the main issues to consider for children with emotional and behavioural difficulties?

In an excellent guide to ICT and special educational needs (Bates 1997), Jeff Hughes, a chartered educational psychologist, is quoted as saying that 'One of the best strategies is to involve the child with [emotional and behavioural difficulties] in positive and rewarding activities. Computers can help create the kind of active and motivating environment in which the learner will experience success.'

The computer provides a non-threatening environment, because children can interact solely with the computer if they wish. They can make mistakes, but can also correct them, without any adult or child making judgements about them. By using the computer, children are able to improve the presentation of their work, which will, in turn, increase their self-esteem when the finished product is of an equal standard to many other children's work in the classroom. Another activity that might engage children with emotional and behavioural difficulties is working with floor robots, which again can be an individual activity that requires working through, and only needs to be demonstrated when the procedure they have written is successful.

The quality of the finished product is of great importance with this group of children, so strategies should be devised that will support them in achieving this. Perhaps their printing can be finally produced on a colour printer, or they can be encouraged to make use of spell checking software and word banks either on screen or on an overlay keyboard, so that the activities, while still challenging, are not so difficult that the children quickly become demotivated. A series of short tasks, with short-term targets and pupil outcomes, is more likely to maintain motivation.

In *Using IT to Support Learners with Emotional and Behavioural Difficulties* (Holt 1998), Laurie Bush and Gill Ingold provide an extremely useful analysis comparing the characteristics and needs of children who have emotional or behavioural difficulties with the support that can be offered to them by using ICT. Impatience, for example, can be countered by the quick results and tangible rewards that computers can provide, and children's need for personal space is satisfied by them sitting in front of their own computers. The need that these children have to maintain an image of being uninterested in learning can be countered by the high status and prestige that ICT often has among their peer group, and their fear and low tolerance of failure can be alleviated by the computer offering small steps, reinforcement and repeated tries with no evidence of failure. Here we have a very clear analysis of the needs of a particular group of children and how ICT can satisfy them, but although the work is done from the perspective of the child with emotional or behavioural difficulties, it applies to any child who has one or another of these characteristics, which is almost certainly the entire school population.

What are the main issues to consider for children with profound and multiple learning difficulties?

Children with profound and multiple learning difficulties need to be considered very much on an individual basis, and often will not be taught in mainstream primary classrooms. However, the main power of the computer as far as this group of children is concerned is its ability to produce ever-changing bright images and sound effects, which respond due to interactions that the children make with the computer.

The ways in which children do interact with the computer are very much decided on an individual basis, depending on the nature of the child's difficulties, but as has been discussed throughout this chapter, there are a very wide range of input devices that could be used.

Are there lessons that can be learned from ICT use with children with special educational needs for all primary-aged children?

Although this chapter has looked at the particular ways in which ICT can help children with special educational needs, it would be wrong to assume that these would be of interest only to teachers who are involved with such children. There is clearly a continuum of abilities and interests that ICT can support, and many, if not most, of the approaches suggested are applicable to all ages and abilities. The overlay keyboard, for example, was designed for use in factories to prevent dirt from engineers' fingers from clogging up conventional keyboards. People then saw how a keyboard of this type might assist children with some physical disability, but then rapidly identified how it could be used by children with a wide range of special educational needs. Subsequently, it seemed to be an ideal introduction to allow young children to interact with computers, and is now extensively used in nursery, reception and Key Stage 1 classrooms. ICT is incredibly flexible, and in analysing what it can do we must avoid categorising particular elements as suitable for 'this' or 'that' type of child. In many cases its power enables the children themselves to decide what they want to do, and in that sense the teacher becomes a facilitator, ensuring the children have the physical means to interact with the computer, but allowing the children themselves to make use of its power.

How can ICT help with gifted and talented children?

The teacher clearly needs to design motivating and challenging tasks carefully, to support exceptional children in developing the sophisticated ICT skills and techniques that they will need in order to engage with complex and varied programs, but the versatility of the computer can give these children enormous opportunities to experiment and develop their ICT capability to the very highest level. For example, most people use only 20 per cent of a word processor's functionality, so there is plenty of scope for experimentation. They need to be encouraged to be autonomous learners. The only issue that you as a teacher have is to avoid being complacent with the very high quality of work that children may be producing, and continually to challenge them to achieve more and more, even though you might be aware that they are using some of the features of the computer that you did not know existed. It is very important that they are not just asked to do more work all of a very similar nature. Give them opportunities to be creative and utilise the power of the ICT facilities that are accessible to them. Using digital video is likely to be a very motivating type of activity for this group of children.

How can ICT help to support inclusive practice?

Some children may be very happy to work by themselves on a computer, while others will learn much better in a group environment. Ensure that you provide a range of different learning experiences to cater for these different kinds of learners.

Make sure the materials you use are culturally diverse. Using Encarta as an encyclopaedia all the time might provide a rather white, Western-based outlook on issues. Consider using Africana – Microsoft's CD-ROM for the black community – sometimes (www.africana.com). There are also multilingual word processors and web translation engines available for community languages.

There are many more ways in which the work in your school can be made more inclusive, and details of these are available on the inclusion website (http://inclusion.ngfl.gov.uk).

Main teaching issues

■ Think about inclusion for all the children you teach; they will all have special needs of some sort.

■ Different forms of communication can open different channels of learning for the child.

■ Make sure that the context is appropriate for the age of the child concerned.

Avoid

■ Using the computer solely for one type of activity.

References

Ager, R. (1997) *Curriculum Bank: Design and Technology at Key Stage Two*. Leamington Spa: Scholastic.

Barrett, J. and Underwood, J. (1997) 'Beyond numeracy', in J. Underwood and J. Brown (eds) *Integrated Learning Systems: Potential into Practice*, 67–78. Oxford: Heinemann.

Bates, R. (1997) *Special Educational Needs: a Practical Guide to IT and Special Educational Needs*. Oxford: RM.

BECTa (2003a) *Primary Schools – ICT and Standards*. Coventry: BECTa.

BECTa (2003b) *Entitlement to ICT in Primary English*. Coventry: BECTa.

BECTa (2003c) *Entitlement to ICT in Primary Mathematics*. Coventry: BECTa.

BECTa (2003d) *Entitlement to ICT in Primary Art and Design*. Coventry: BECTa.

BECTa (2003e) *Entitlement to ICT in Primary Design and Technology*. Coventry: BECTa.

BECTa (2003f) *Entitlement to ICT in Primary Geography*. Coventry: BECTa.

BECTa (2003g) *Entitlement to ICT in Primary History*. Coventry: BECTa.

BECTa (2003h) *Entitlement to ICT in Primary Music*. Coventry: BECTa.

BECTa (2003i) *Entitlement to ICT in Religious Education*. Coventry: BECTa.

Campbell, B. (1989) 'Multiplying intelligence in the classroom', *On the Beam*, **9**, 2.

DfEE (1997) *Excellence in Schools*. London: The Stationery Office.

DfES (2003a) *Towards a Unified e-Learning Strategy (Consultation Document)*. Nottingham: DfES.

DfES (2003b) *Fulfilling the Potential: Transforming Teaching and Learning through ICT in Schools*. Nottingham: DfES.

Gardner, H. (1993) *Frames of Mind: The Theory of Multiple Intelligences*. London: Fontana Press.

Gardner, J. (1997) 'ILS and under-achievers', in J. Underwood and J. Brown (eds) *Integrated Learning Systems: Potential into Practice*, 88–102. Oxford: Heinemann.

Holt, G. (1998) *Using IT to Support Learners with Emotional and Behavioural Difficulties*. Coventry: NCET.

Kaku, M. (1998) *Visions: How Science Will Revolutionize the 21st Century and Beyond*. Oxford: Oxford University Press.

Lewis, A. (1997) 'ILS and pupils with special educational needs', in J. Underwood and J. Brown (eds) *Integrated Learning Systems: Potential into Practice*, 103–17. Oxford: Heinemann.

PrimaryViewPoint (2003) *Key Stage 2 Science*. Telford: PrimaryViewPoint.

QCA (2000) *Curriculum Guidance for the Foundation Stage*. London: QCA.

QCA/DfES (2000) *Information and Communication Technology: Scheme of Work for Key Stages 1 and 2*. London: QCA.

QCA/DfES (2003) *Information and Communication Technology (Scheme of Work for Key Stages 1 and 2) Teachers' Guide (Revised)*. London: QCA.

Rodrigues, S. (1997) 'Able students working in ILS environments', in J. Underwood and J. Brown (eds) *Integrated Learning Systems: Potential into Practice*, 118–26. Oxford: Heinemann.

Somekh, B. (1997) 'Classroom investigations: exploring and evaluating how IT can support learning', in B. Somekh and N. Davis (eds) *Using Information Technology Effectively in Teaching and Learning*, 114–26. London: Routledge.

Teacher Training Agency (1998) *The Use of Information and Communication Technology in Subject Teaching*. London: TTA.

Underwood, J. and Brown, J. (eds) (1997) *Integrated Learning Systems: Potential into Practice*. Oxford: Heinemann.

Underwood, J., Cavendish, S., Dowling, S., Lawson, T. (1997) 'Beyond numeracy', in J. Underwood and J. Brown (eds) *Integrated Learning Systems: Potential into Practice*, 54–66. Oxford: Heinemann.

Vygotsky, L. S. (1978) *Mind in Society: the Development of Higher Psychological Processes*. Cambridge, MA: Harvard University Press.

Whitebread, D. (1997) 'Developing children's problem-solving', in A. McFarlane (ed.) *Information Technology and Authentic Learning*, 13–37. London: Routledge.

Index